Dorothy & Omer
Happy Anniversary
1997

our love

Joyce & Dave

good land

good land

My Life as a Farm Boy

BRUCE BAIR

STEERFORTH PRESS

SOUTH ROYALTON, VERMONT

For information about permission to reproduce
selections from this book, write to:
Steerforth Press L.C., P.O. Box 70, South Royalton, Vermont 05068.

Library of Congress Cataloging-in-Publication Data
Bair, Bruce, 1944-
Good land : memoir of a farmer's son / Bruce Bair. — 1st ed.
p. cm.
ISBN 1-883642-34-5 (alk. paper)
1. Bair, Bruce, 1944- . 2. Farmers — Kansas — Goodland — Biography.
I. Title.
S417.B215A3   1997
630'.92—dc21
[B]   96-48710
CIP

Manufactured in the United States of America

FIRST EDITION

contents

good land   1

bairs   4

carlsons   9

a farm is just land   12

the big drought   15

the meadowlark   18

white-tailed jackrabbits   21

on death and atheism   24

lynn   27

iron   31

tractors   35

one way   41

school (ha!)   46

the pool   54

julene   58

vacations   62

childhood friends   66

discipline   70

sex   74

hired hands   78

sheep   86

our place — the other place   91

i try farming   96

sugar beets   106

werk   111

a wrestling match to the death   120

off the farm   131

we get mellow   135

i'm fine. why shouldn't i be?   140

julene brought him out of it   144

clark   147

julie   152

mother   155

the big tractor   162

ron and nyla   170

my pickup   174

harold's pickup   176

another funeral   179

a song scattered in the wind   187

good land

We would like to think differently, but the history of the Plains farmer is as thin as the soil of a hillside tilled a hundred years, which is about how long the Plains have been producing wheat. Our farmers didn't even lay out the fields. Surveyors did that, and only after it was all laid out and safe did the farmers arrive. The greatest discomfort the bulk of our early settlers experienced in getting here was in stepping off the train. Then the hardships began. They were in Kansas, in towns laid out on bare prairie by land speculators. Most of these towns evaporated in a year or two. Optimism and Exhultanea blew away or burnt up, but Eureka and Paradise and Gem remain. Some of the names twist the tongue so teasingly, they are pleasures — Wynona, Bucyrus, Ada, and Faith. But most often, the towns were Colbies, Oakleys, or Atwoods, good solid names land dealers could live with. At least they picked a name for my town that fit. They called it Goodland.

Our farmstead is nine miles west (you turn north at Ruleton), six miles north, two miles west, two-and-a-half miles north, and another half-mile west of Goodland. My mother has given the directions so many times to custom cutters, tire busters, cattle brokers, implement salesmen and others, it's like a litany to her. She forgets to give people time to write it down. How could anyone not know how to get there? The farmstead is on a little clay knob, and because of big grain bins (full most of the time) and an old red block silo it is visible from the west for miles.

All around the knob lies our farm. The farmstead itself sits on a half-section. (A section is one square a mile on a side and contains 640 acres.) Aside from the buildings in one corner, and a forty-acre patch broken out bordering another man's land, it's all grass. But oh, glory! To the west of this is a whole flat section, three quarters of it developed for irrigation. Bordering this is another quarter-section, also developed, which we have called all my life the "quarter west of the section." To the north are two more sections, containing three more irrigated circles. A half-section of wheat land lies a half mile east of the farmstead. This is the bulk of it — in all, about four square miles — but there's more. Slightly separated is a half-section of rough farmland along Beaver Creek which we call No Man's Land. Adjacent to No Man's Land is an entirely different world, six quarters (960 acres) of grass. A few odd corners of it are fenced off and farmed, but this is prairie as virgin as it gets in Kansas. This grass raised sheep for years and now is used sporadically to pasture cattle, but it has always been treated well. Ancient windmills pump along the creek into ten-foot-deep concrete and limestone tanks my grandfather built. On this part of the farm one can imagine buffalo grazing. It can be a pretty place. And it's all good land.

To understand how good requires a little geography. Travel twenty miles in any direction from Goodland and you won't find a hill a hundred feet high or a valley a hundred feet deep. The Smoky Hill River, which runs east of town, does have a few breaks around it and a few bluffs overlooking it. Sometimes it even has water in it.

The bulk of the drainage in Sherman County, forty miles by forty miles, a precise square on the Colorado border, is provided by the multitudinous branches of Beaver and Sappa Creeks. Not enough water has run down any of the Beaver's branches or the Sappa's in the million years or so they've been there to dig a decent valley. The geologists say that the whole country lies atop an alluvial fan from the Rocky Mountains. Eons ago, the fan was covered with blow dirt from somewhere else. It's called loess. Any place that has it is usually farming heaven. In our county, it's thirty feet deep in places, shallower in others. The underlying fan is mostly gravel and sand, and under that, limestone. The creeks have managed to dig down to the top of the sand. In another million years, they might make it to the limestone.

The sand and gravel underlying the loess ranges in depth from several feet to hundreds. Over the ages, rainfall has trickled into the porous sands, forming the Ogallala aquifer, a vast lake of pure underground water. Hydrologists say that in places, rivers run under the ground, though the country above is usually parched. It may be the best and purest water in the world and it makes the country livable. It is this underground lake which waters our corn. Two feet of topsoil above the loess make the country farmable. And no trees and no rocks.

bairs

Behind every farm is a grandfather. I suppose in the East, great- and great-great-grandfathers float over the country like unseen ghosts, checking the corn, smelling the tobacco, hoeing the cotton. But in western Kansas, where our farm is located, we haven't been here that long. Grandfathers most often founded the farm. They were grandfathers herding Herefords, planting wheat, randily siring dynasties if they could.

My grandfather was slope-nosed and sprouted unpruned eyebrows. I'd like to believe his eyes were blue, but memory fails after so many years. He once told me I wasn't worth a cunt full of cold water and slapped me on the ass with a piece of stiff No. 9 wire, which raised a welt. Younger grandchildren crawled on his lap and were rewarded with a nickel.

His wife, Maud, was usually in the kitchen, cooking. The flesh under her arms flapped when she rolled noodle dough. She never bought a grocery store chicken in her life, and when she cooked the yard varieties, she left the feet on.

But Grandfather's early history has always been fuzzy to me. The story goes that he came out of Nebraska in the 1920s with a couple of nag horses and settled around St. Francis. Somehow, and in a very few years, he'd traded those nag horses up and owned sixty quarter-sections of land, or about fifteen square miles. A friend's mother once told me that when he went to the courthouse to pay his annual taxes, he'd reel off the legal description of each of the quarters. The clerk would look up the tax, and add the totals on a pad. When she was done, he would write a check. Once, she said, he returned to the courthouse crushed with embarrassment. He'd forgotten one.

His name was Ferdinand Fernando Bair.

How he got a name like that, no one seems to know. His brothers, scattered over most parts of the earth, had more conventional names and were said to be successful, but I never met them. Dad talked about them sometimes. Aaron, from California, looked a lot like Ferd. My father told me Bairs lived in Montana. Shortly after he married my mother, Jasmin, he visited them in White Sulphur Springs. This is how I learned that one of my female relatives rolled smokes from a bag of Bull Durham.

Of my grandfather's antecedents I know little more except for an old family legend. His father, my great-grandfather, lived with Ferd and Maud for a time. A meaner, more cantankerous man never lived, my father says. There's a picture of him somewhere, a skinny, fierce-looking man with a white, straight beard falling on his chest. And because he was mean and old, his grandchildren teased him unmercifully, once painting his beard barn red. Most children would have gotten a whipping for doing something like that, my father said. But the Bair children were whipped more or less randomly, or when white spots were found under their fingernails. Maud believed that meant children were lying.

In addition to this there is a chart made up by my Aunt Edith. Somewhere is a woman named Imhampuk, so I can probably claim some Indian blood. William Least Heat Moon has nothing on me.

My grandmother Maud's family was more immediate. We were packed off at least once a year to see my great-grandmother. She was one of those thin women who age without weakening into their nineties. When I was about six or seven, the family was conducted to her deathbed. One by one, she called for the great-grandchildren. One eye opened and a thin claw-like hand reached out to grasp ours. She said something to me in a husking voice. Her breath was bad and she rattled, and I couldn't understand her. We were being given a lesson about duty as basic to family and farming as pig-slopping. Family was not to be abandoned on the deathbed. Our parents didn't worry about damaging our tender psyches by subjecting us to such a scene. Death was as much a part of life as growing up and it was usually a well-attended family affair. We were watched closely to see how we reacted to this tragedy, while this creature of skin, bones and liver spots grasped each of our hands and whispered unintelligible garble in our ears. One thing was clear. Great-Grandma knew who each of us was, and none could escape until she had touched every one of us. Once we were released onto the hospital lawn, we stood about in clumps with our heads down for a while, absorbing the lesson of death. Then someone got out a softball.

Of course, she recovered, and lived another few years with Aunt Rosie Stump. When she at last died, it was quickly and without further fanfare. We may have attended the funeral. I remember the funerals of all the rest — the coffins and the obsequious morticians. But I don't remember hers. The image of her yellowing in the hospital bed remains too strong.

She lived perhaps the way people were meant to in Nebraska, with chickens and maybe a milk cow, even in town. Mom called her house a shack. It had no indoor plumbing,

which to Jasmin was a trial. We had by that time progressed beyond that, but just barely.

Mother would mutter about it on the drive to Nebraska.
"Oh, I just hate going there, there's no toilets." But she hadn't
forgotten we'd only had our bathroom a year or two. She guessed
she could get by.

"At least it don't have black widow spiders," I'd chirrup from
the rear. I was already like my father, always probing people for a
reaction, but I was getting my rises out of them in a different way.
With a joke. I haven't changed much.

"I hope I get the toy section," I'd follow up. I actually remember using the Montgomery Ward catalog for such purposes.
Our outhouse was still in use as a second bathroom, and at that
time, outhouse jokes comprised 90 percent of the repertoire of
Plains humorists, and I was no different. The toy section was a
prize because I had something to read. My brother sat beside me,
already graduated to the women's underwear section, his feet
barely touching the floorboards of the big Chrysler, looking
straight ahead and acting as if I couldn't have possibly said anything funny.

Mixed up in this memory, in the haloed glow of childhood,
is a snuffling, friendly bulldog and a goldfish pond. And good
food, tall sunflowers and hollyhocks, and my grandmother's
brothers, Jum and Limpy, both still legendary shockers, and in
their day, bindle stiffs. One was walleyed and the other limped.
They talked sotto voce — why, no one knows. Everyone in our
family agreed, there had never been anything like them. How
they sounded is impossible to describe, though I'll give it a stab.
They sounded like a bearing wearing out halfway between Wray
and Hagler.

My grandfather must have died in the early 1960s, in his
eighties. He won the prize for being the oldest in attendance at
one of our family reunions. He died in an easy chair after chasing

Herefords through the pasture. In his ancient old age, he paid cash at the White Motor Company for a Cadillac. My father shook his head at the extravagance of it.

Grandfather's prow-like nose stuck out of the coffin. His hands were crossed, and his bushy eyebrows seemed wilder than ever. He looked like he was sleeping. My father was in shock, the only time I have ever seen him that way, but I expect I will know how he felt soon enough.

This was my second or third funeral so I knew the routine. I was supposed to be quiet. I was supposed to be good. I was not to get grass stains on the knees of my gray pants.

Grandmother Maud had died years before of a stroke. She was cooking and guiltily lay down, complaining of a headache. A few minutes later, she was dead. As she lay in her coffin, I slipped a cereal box sheriff's star into her pocket, and I imagine it is still there, lying among her bones. She looked as fat and friendly in the coffin as she had in life, except her nose stuck up. Maybe it's only the angle, but I have come to think that in death, the face subsides quickly from the nose no matter what the morticians do. By now, I have lived long enough to have seen many noses sticking out of coffins. Sometimes, I dream of noses sticking out of the ground, Bairs planted like so many potatoes in the good land.

carlsons

To find a family more cockamamie than the Bairs, Harold, my father, had only to go a few miles straight east and cross the creek to the Carlsons. My mother-to-be, Jasmin, lived there.

"She had me pawing the earth," he said.

It is easy to see why from early pictures, probably taken by Jasmin's older brother, Leonard. She and her sister Helen are dressed up in bandanna tops and shorts and posed against barns and old rock piles. They were as lithe as swans and pretty as meadowlarks.

Grandmother Elizabeth Carlson lived a long time. Most of us called her Lizzie. Like her husband, John, she had emigrated from Scandinavia when she was a small child. By the time I knew her she was so old I couldn't imagine anyone older. But you did not screw around with her. When I was sent to Goodland to help her, she dosed me with a tonic that she made out of water and old nails kept in a gallon jar and sent me out to rake up weeds in the garden. It was hard to concentrate because it was a garden you could get lost in — birdbaths and multitudes of tall old-time flowers, and iris (her and Mother's favorite flower), and millions of earthworms and sow bugs. How could anybody get anything done?

"Any job worth doing is worth doing well," she would lecture. She really was a grump. But when it came to me, Grandma was a pushover. Out would come the fig cookies. She'd even put down a small glass of fortified Mogen David wine. Grandma always had plenty of wine. We knew how much she drank because Mother did her shopping. It took a weekly trip to the liquor store to keep Grandma happy.

What was funny about the Carlsons was their drawl. Why they spoke that way no one knows but all of them did it. Leonard did it best. "I j-u-u-u-st don't kn-o-o-o-o-o-w," he would say. Through the years Mother has gotten rid of most of the accent. Harold teased it out of her, but under stress she'll revert, and then she "j-u-u-u-st couldn't s-a-a-a-a-y."

But there was more to it than that. All of the Carlsons spoke as if they were awaiting a crushing blow. Grandmother, it seems, was often depressed. Her house in town was bleak and dark, and contrasted so crazily with the garden it was almost schizophrenic. The bathroom was hung with hot water bottles and tubes and syringes for colonics. You entered it through Grandma's bedroom, filled with dark and looming furniture, and a wardrobe of black dresses with ruffled fronts. Her room always smelled of medicine.

Elizabeth and John Oliver Carlson managed to make babies over three decades despite not liking each other very much. The children were Irene, Emma, Ruth, John, Helen, and Leonard, born in that order. Mother is the youngest. Mother has taken on the job of writing the family history and relates that Elizabeth once accused John Oliver of "cutting down a perfectly good bed to fit the school teacher." It is not known if John Oliver ever committed adultery with a schoolmarm, but Elizabeth, a true Carlson, was likely happier to accuse her husband of something he hadn't done than she would have been if she had caught him in the act. John Oliver made a farm of it though, and in his later years took on businesses in Goodland. He died in a narrow bed in a Spartan rooming house. The Carlsons were Scandinavians, dark, brooding, crushed by the Lutheran Church, carrying the world on their shoulders, afraid of themselves, and paying cash "by Got."

Elizabeth and Jasmin knew the value of a good man. Harold was five years older than Jasmin. His father, Ferdinand, was almost a Sherman County farming legend. Besides, Harold was educated. Somehow, during the Depression, he'd gotten through four years of college, and he had a great job testing dairy cattle for brucellosis. And he was strong and damned good-looking. In comparison with the dour Carlsons, he must have seemed devil-may-care.

Soon after they were married, he quit the job and bought a farm of his own, paying a fair price for some of Ferdinand's land. Then the great tragedy which all Carlsons await, struck. Jasmin's brother John was killed by lightning while driving a tractor. Leonard couldn't handle the farm, and Lizzie had already moved to town, so Harold took over on shares and now he had two farms. They moved into the big red-roofed house with the second floor porch John Oliver had built, the home Mother grew up in. She made it light inside and the gardens were beautiful, and for the most part, she stopped drawling.

a farm is just land

A farm is just land. Ours must have once been prime hunting grounds. As late as the 1930s, people picked up arrowheads by the jarful. I've found dozens myself. Indians lived here for ten thousand years. In the 1950s, it was still possible for a small boy fascinated with artifacts to find a stone gristmill with two smooth stones in its bowl.

The county contained hundreds of buffalo wallows. Wallows were made by buffalo rolling in mud in low spots. When they walked away, they took the mud with them. Eventually, they made flat-bottomed, temporary lakes, some as large as forty acres. Rains filled these, and the ducks followed. Farmers found the wallows a nuisance, and farmed through them. These ponds are still around but the bottoms are ruined and they dry up too quickly for the ducks to make much use of them.

It must have been rich. It was pristine until the first railroad was built. It was to railheads on the progressing lines that Texas cowboys drove cattle. But the open range didn't last long. The surveyors who won the west had already laid the country out in squares and the homesteaders came. Immediately they began breaking out the prairie in 160-acre pieces, a half-mile on a side. Now, instead of buffalo grass cut by a few spring-fed creeks, and dotted with glistening round lakes surrounded by reeds, a checkerboard of cultivated land had evolved, yellow and brown and green from the air.

All this went slowly at first, until the 1920s wheat boom. The new mechanical contrivances, the steam tractor and thresher, and the twelve gang plows finished most of it off. Inexplicably, a few squares of good flat land were left in grass up to the early 1960s. But these are gone too, eaten up in the irrigation boom. Boom and bust has always been the economic cycle of the High Plains.

With the topsoil exposed the springs went fast. Mother remembers fishing in Beaver Creek, which cut through a corner of the old Carlson farm. Now the nearest permanent water in it is fifty miles downstream from her old fishing hole. Runoff from farmland silted the springs shut. Irrigation got most of the rest later. From the air, circles can be seen inscribed in thousands of the squares. The circles are made by central pivot irrigation systems sucking from that big Ogallala aquifer. The cornfields can be like swamps and twice I've seen a hatch of dragonflies from one of them at the moment kestrels are migrating.

Kestrels feasting on dragonflies are an example of one way big farming and irrigation have skewed the ecology. Dragonflies in such abundance could never have hatched out of dry buffalo grass, but a swampy cornfield is ideal for them. We have birds and animals we didn't used to have, and some of the animals and birds I grew up with are gone. But some grass remains and so one kind of jackrabbit survives. The prairie dog still ekes out an existence, popping out of his hole with as much impertinence as ever, and farmers respond by salting the earth with cyanide-laced barley.

Most of the land is still cultivated dryland style, which helps, because hundreds of miles of weed-choked barbed wire fences, gullies, and road ditches are left and provide cover. The deer and the antelope still play. Especially, the deer. They like irrigated corn. The sun shines most of the time. And you can walk wherever you like. It pays to like wind.

the big drought

But most of the grass is gone now. When the big drought comes, we may miss the grass. Grass is the seed nature plants to save the land from wind. Drought is the sword hanging over us at all times. It may have been the reason the Scandinavian Carlsons drawled so. A calamity is always waiting for us. To live on the Plains is to live with the knowledge that drought could wipe us out at any time.

Scientists warn us about it. They take core samples of trees, when they can find them, and carbon-date wood taken from Indian sites, and study annual rings and make estimates. Or they look at pollen composition in sediments, and guess 2000 B.C. was a very dry year. They warn that the whole country sometimes dries up for decades. They don't call the Sandhills of Nebraska and Colorado sand hills for nothing. They're dunes, plastered down with grass so recently there's hardly any topsoil. Three years of rainfalls below ten inches would be enough to wipe out the High Plains. Two years would probably do the job. The cattle would all be gone. What few that were left would be living on stickers, just as happened in 1919 after a single year of drought. Any wheat farmer carrying debt would go under. And the irrigators would pump so frantically they'd lower the water table another ten feet, hastening the day when the Ogallala aquifer is gone. Yet the scientists say sometimes droughts on the High Plains can go on for a hundred years.

We've already had plenty of experience with little dry spells. I mentioned 1919; everyone's heard of the Dirty Thirties; I'm old enough to remember 1956, when the farm received 9.53 inches of rain. The sheep pastures went, and the sheep were sold. The wheat crop failed, and even barley and millet wouldn't grow. Harold and Mother fought. My father wanted no money spent. What the hell was she supposed to feed us, she yelled — jackrabbits?

He stomped off. My father figured it was the Depression all over again and we were in it for the long haul. What else was he to think? Stepping out of the milk barn with my pail, I saw him running toward me. He had a look of resignation on his face I hadn't seen before. He blocked the barn door. Only then did I notice something different about the air. It had a brown color, and the sun was an orange disk. Then it hit, and the air was so filled with blowing dust and grit and sand, we couldn't see five feet. It got dark. "Dirt storm," my father said.

It only happened about five times that year. In the stores, merchants kept sheets over the merchandise and in our house mother swept up the dust and threw it over the edge of the second story porch in a scoop shovel. "G-o-o-o-d d-a-a-mned dirt," she drawled. The government stepped in and formed something called the soil bank which paid farmers so much an acre to simply quit and let things go back to grass. We had disaster payments and soil bank payments and scraped by. It rained that fall or the next year, but Harold had to borrow the money to buy the next sheep herd. He had been wiped out.

We're constantly fed propaganda that a Dust Bowl can't happen again because of our modern farming practices. Under the new methods a lot more crop debris from the previous year is left on top. This is supposed to prevent the soil from blowing. But only a few years ago, in March, after an open winter and no rain, an eighty-mile-an-hour cold north wind hit while I was standing outside the *Hays Daily News* office talking to a photographer, Charles Riedel. He was gaping like a boy in the doorway of a milk barn.

"Don't you know what that is, Charlie?" I asked. He looked blank. "It's a goddamned dirt storm."

Just this year and last we've had a little taste of it. The papers were talking about the driest ten months in history, but history only means the hundred or so years records have been kept. In May, after it was too late for wheat and the price of a good feeder calf plunged below fifty cents a pound in the Texas panhandle, it rained. We got seven inches in about two weeks and the ground soaked up every drop of it. It always rains, doesn't it?

the meadowlark

Drought — we're always looking over our shoulders at it and up in the sky for it to end. Why would anyone live here at all? But there are compensations.

On the first subfreezing morning of the year, the new black pup licked the grass, trying to figure out what frost was. I came to a stop, the dog came to a stop, then she bounced off, her back undulating. I figured she was dancing to an Irish reel I couldn't quite hear. The cold clear air rendered everything so intensely it was like being high. Then I did hear it. The meadowlark.

The wind brought the song to me in tatters. Still, it was unmistakable. The black pup listened, four feet planted and tail and ears erect. I had been brooding over a deadline, but suddenly I wasn't worried at all. I was part of it, the air and the land — just another Plains creature without a clock in my soul, and I was grinning. The bird made me happy. How little a Plainsman can get by with. That bird would be heading for Texas soon and I would have to trudge through another winter without him. Even that made me happy — good joke that bird plays.

In my youth, the meadowlark was the only animal besides livestock that wasn't fair game. Dad shot kingbirds hovering over the elm trees just to hear the satisfying thump on clay. I pumped so many BBs into barn pigeons that they eventually fell from the weight. Such carnage was acceptable. Still, whenever I trotted off with my .22, Mother told me, "Don't you dare shoot any meadowlarks."

I could make myself draw a bead on the yellow breast of a meadowlark on a fence post, but I couldn't make myself shoot. If I did, somehow I always missed. (Yes, I confess, at one time or another, a dead meadowlark may have reached my hand, but it was only for scientific perusal.) I think they'd be good eating. They have a hefty breast. It's the song and the yellow-breasted jauntiness of the bird that keeps them out of the pot.

Red-winged blackbirds and yellow-headed orioles land by the thousands in the milo fields, but they eat grain. Neat yellow kingbirds fight and caw most ungraciously. We never hesitated to gauge these birds twelve ways, to see how many we could get in one shot.

But meadowlarks are different. They have no bad habits. They sing alone, like a boy on a tractor.

You can't get enough in one shot to matter, anyway, since they're solitary. And it's not sporting to shoot something that sits on a fence post ten feet away, waiting for it.

Why they sit there is no particular mystery. The bright breasted males are warbling for sex. The drabber hens are harder to find. A lot of larking goes on, and soon there are speckled eggs. Then the males hop right back on the fence posts and keep on singing. Biologists say it's territorial. I say it's summer.

Go to any prairie art exhibit and you'll find a painting of the bird, sitting on its post. Listen carefully here, for what is going on is important. Think of us as an experiment. Take Caucasian folk and scatter them widely across arid farmlands. Have them speak all sorts of foreign languages and become, in three generations, Americans. Allow the survivors to farm.

Then go to the exhibit.

Here are what Plainsmen pause before.

Old windmills, tumbledown barns, pheasants, rusted tools hung on board fences, Herefords on hillsides, and meadowlarks. What is important is the sparse symbolism. The mind of a landsman is serene. He's learned even if he's smart enough to do it that complicated thought is a waste of time. Because it won't change the weather. It won't get corn delivered to a feed yard. It won't weld a broken bean knife blade. No matter how driven a farmer is, how filled his mind is with wheat markets and bank interest rates, or what a bully bastard he might be, keeping on top of sixteen central pivots and two thousand head of cattle, the Plains eventually seep into the worst of them. The sparseness and the space make them humble or they are fools. It's happened even to my father.

The symbols which anchor us are simple. God and Jesus for most, the way things weather and fall, pump and work, and bless the Hereford cow — these are enough.

Sometimes a Plainsman will even buy a painting, though buying art is embarrassing.

"What you gonna do with that, Jake?"

"Why, hang it on my wall."

He hides it quickly behind the seat of his pickup so no one else will see. Fifty dollars for a picture — whoever heard of such a thing?

The only excuse he can make at home while dangling the picture from his hand is that he just thought it was pretty.

"Well, here," he says, and hands it to his wife.

"Why, it's a meadowlark," she says, and gives him a big kiss because there's not been flowers for decades and she looks for a place to hang it.

Who doesn't like meadowlarks?

white-tailed jackrabbits

Dad, educated in the thirties, a possessor of college "chums," was thoroughly indoctrinated in the philosophy of "doing." His father drilled it into him. The colleges he attended instilled it further. The philosophy of the times also included the concept of "pep," a sort of mindless civic pride which today is called positive thinking. Doers were supposed to be the antidote for the Depression, but it took pep. If you just worked hard and didn't think bad thoughts, even during a dirt storm, everything would work out. As we drove to work, Harold would point out the successes and failures of other farmers as he saw them.

"He's a doer," he'd say, or, "He's kind of a doer," or "He does it sometimes." These gradations are incomplete. Every time we drove past Wilmot Price's beautifully landscaped and immaculate farmstead, he'd say, "Will not." Wilmot didn't put out enough acres in Harold's opinion.

No doubt exists as to which classification Dad fits into. He's a doer.

What he did was build a four thousand-acre, diversified farm, the envy of the neighbors. If they don't envy it, they are simply brainless. To do it, he farmed clean for decades. So have all the survivors. A growing weed is a pump sucking moisture out of the soil.

But he wonders what happened to the white-tailed jackrabbit.

He called me in Montana once. I'd mentioned the rabbits had turned white, so it must be winter. "They don't know what color to be in the spring. They get blotchy."

"You got those things up there? What color's the tail?"

"White."

"White-tailed jackrabbits, huh?"

"So?"

"We used to have those. But you don't see them anymore."

"Why would that be?" I ask gently. "Could it be because all the grass is plowed up?"

"Well, maybe," he says. But it's not an important point to him. "Do you suppose a fella could catch some of those?" He's suggesting the fellow could be me. "I wonder how you could get them down here? Put them in a crate, maybe? A fella might get them started up again."

"I don't think they have the habitat. They live on grasslands here, big ones."

"Huh?" He doesn't get it, or has decided to ignore me when I make insane comments about how habitat supports fauna. A damned jackrabbit ought to be able to live anywhere.

"I'd like to see them around again, damn it. How would a fella go about getting them? Why don't you look into that?"

"Sure," I say. I'm not going to tell him that catching a jackrabbit is probably a federal offense. Such laws are nonsense to Plainsmen, ignored like the prohibition against drinking Coors while driving pickup trucks.

Dad's a doer. If he ever really turns his mind to it, he'll bring back the white-tailed jackrabbit without me. He'll find some way to creep-feed them so they don't need so damned much pasture. It would be a good project, if he ever retires. But white-tailed jackrabbits are only a transitory wish, the stray thought of a man busy farming who sometimes longs for the way it used to be.

At eighty, Dad drives around in a big red air-conditioned Ford pickup. It's a dandy. I ride around with him two or three times a year. He digs me out of my lair, usually on the pretext of some farm crisis. He says he's going to put me to work, but usually talks to me most of the time.

The big pasture south of the house is all good friable farmland, a good place to stock white-tailed jackrabbits. Harold has threatened to break it out for years, but hasn't done it. Maybe what stops him is that the pasture is the linchpin of a diversified farm. Good grass, the cheapest of feeds, and close to home, where the stock can be gotten in case of a storm. But he knows leaving such good land unfarmed is an anachronism. Cattle are always iffy. When you pencil it out, wheat makes more money.

It's a question like white-tailed jackrabbits he's twisted around in his mind for years, maybe seven one way and five the other. "Don't let go of that grass," he's thinking. "Wheat could go totally to hell."

I know he sees a wheat field there sometimes, or maybe two irrigated circles. It's something that after fifty years a doer didn't do. Besides, sometimes kit foxes den out there. Those foxes make him grin. He shuts off the pickup. It's quiet. A meadowlark sings. He doesn't say a thing, but his eyes flick toward the fence post. He looks old and tired and the flesh is receding from his nose.

on death and atheism

On a farm, you see lots of dead things. Lambs are stillborn, ewes get struck by lightning, cattle choke on turnip tops unless you can shove them down throats fast enough with a broom handle.

To a boy, death is just one more facet of nature to be studied. Driving in a pickup, we often came upon a pile of bones in a pasture corner. I'd ask Dad what happened.

"Pete dragged those out here after they died in a corral," or "She just laid down and died," or "Goddamned coyotes got her." Coyotes made him look sour. He still hates them.

Death was something I hunkered in front of. In the summer, just after death, the stricken cow or sheep or horse would look asleep if it weren't for the tongue sticking out and the head twisted back. I couldn't count the times I've spotted a sleeping animal on a hill and said, "Look over there. Is there something wrong?"

"It's asleep," my Dad would reply.

It's something older people learn and I came to learn. Death can be seen at long distances.

A childhood reader, I've always been myopic. My father, a Plainsman pure, has always been farsighted. He could pick out a dead sheep lying in the middle of a herd a half-mile away and would drive over immediately to ascertain the cause, usually coyotes, though often sheep, like turtles, roll over in a rut and can't get up again. They'd die that way, from congestion.

After a day or so in the sun a dead animal bloats, and its legs stick straight out like poles. This process continues until the hide of the animal can no longer contain the accumulating gases and the animal deflates — that putrid sigh of death. I know, since often I provoked that sigh. A three-inch Red Ryder pocketknife will always do it, but a sharp stick works fine.

Once deflation has occurred, the bones quickly become outlined under the hide. Eyes ooze and disappear. Pry an animal dead a week over with a board and underneath the hide is already eaten away and the bone visible amid mounds of maggots. All around the carcass will be the signs of birds and animals, coyotes and hawks, which tug at the loose skin and the deliquescing flesh beneath and carry pieces of it away. Even jackrabbits have a carnivorous bent, or maybe they're only after the calcium.

Within a month or two, only the remnants of the hide and bones connected by tendons are left. The stink is almost gone. Within a year, only the bones remain, scattered by animals now, scattered even further by the following summer, and ignored where they lie thereafter. Bleaching occurs, the last red and black carrion beetle drops out of the eye socket, and the horned skull of a steer is wired to the radiator grill of the Power Wagon by a hired hand.

Sometimes, out of the blue, my father has said to me, "When you die, that's it."

"No different from a dog in a ditch?"

"Nope," he says, "no different."

If that is what he really believes, he has no reason to fear, but I can see that now he may be rethinking the matter. Still, on death's door, he refuses to admit it.

The first flare-up of his congestive heart failure occurred in the late summer of 1993. His lungs filled with water and he could barely breathe. Just before he was taken by air ambulance to St. Luke's in Denver, the Lutheran preacher arrived. Father has always been an atheist, though he calls his non-belief "not being a church man."

He knew he was in big trouble and said so. His breath came in gasps.

The preacher wanted to know if he could be placed on the prayer tree.

I've often thought of writing an "Etiquette for Atheists." What is the correct behavior when cornered by a Christian? My father, even in church, refuses to bow his head when the preacher says "let us pray." He stares fiercely around. Although I am not a Christian, I fake it, and bow my head, covertly glancing at others, sometimes even pretty women. The reason my father does not bow his head is simple. He does not want to be a hypocrite.

"No," said my father. "I've never been a church man. That would make me a hypocrite, wouldn't it?"

My father isn't even going to pray on his deathbed.

"We're all hypocrites. That's why we do pray," said the preacher.

"Well, I'm not," said Harold. "That's why I don't." He was gasping for breath.

What a time to be arguing theology, I was thinking.

"Don't you want to be on the prayer tree?" the preacher asked again. He was plaintive, now.

"I guess it couldn't hurt," Dad said. "I could probably use some."

But he only said that because he was sick. He was too tired to argue. And it got rid of the preacher.

lynn

Before 1880, wheat was cut by hand with scythes and bound into bundles. A Works Progress Administration artist painted a version of "Bringing in the Sheaves" as a mural on the walls of our post office. Hefty women in kerchiefs and sack-like brown dresses were bent over in the painted field like stumps, tying up the bundles.

About the time our country was settled, horse-drawn binders became common. If a six-gun won the West, the McCormick binder won the Plains. Every Kansas school boy was taught this at one time. Such vast acreage could never have been scythed and bundled by hand. The binder mechanized those jobs.

It remains an elegant device, which when well oiled and in good repair, cuts wheat almost as quietly as a scythe man must have. A big slatted reel pulls the wheat against the sickle. The sickle is made up of dozens of triangular, three-inch serrated knives driven back and forth by a wobble gear against ledger plates. It works just like scissors. The crop falls on a wide canvas conveyor and is taken to a mechanical knotter.

A man rides on the metal seat, operating levers which raise and lower the sickle and the reel. His foot rests on a pedal which dumps accumulated bundles from a carriage.

I was the boy on the metal seat. Lynn Mann, Dad's friend and hired hand, drove the tractor and fixed the binder when it broke. Harold said he didn't know why Lynn Mann was his friend. He just liked him. All of this was a mystery to me, as Harold disliked drinking and Lynn was a sot.

But Lynn was careful, even when drunk. He drove home from binges in Goodland, averaging four hours to make the thirty-minute trip. At five miles an hour, he explained, he had more allowance for error, but he often drove into the ditch anyway. Sometimes he didn't make it back for weeks, which Dad found to be his greatest failing.

But for Lynn, he'd make allowances. Lynn would show up again, explaining he was broke. He wondered if he could sleep in the trailer.

"I fired you, goddamn it."

But Lynn looked pretty sorry, still shivering from alcohol. He was stooped a little and always wore faded jeans and a faded blue shirt and cowboy boots turned up at the toes and was as natural to the country as the white trunk of a dead cottonwood. He'd been in the war. Since then he'd been drunk. Harold would relent.

The next day we'd go into the trailer and he'd be making coffee for us. They would negotiate a little, and Lynn would go back to work. He crossed his legs and hunched like a cowboy over his coffee. Harold liked to sit in the trailer's only easy chair, leaning back to gulp his. My brother Clark and I usually sat on the couch. Clark, always careful not to sin, didn't drink coffee. We both hoped that that day we'd work with Lynn Mann.

Lynn didn't get mad or throw wrenches or keep pressure on us like Harold did. We got as much done, but it almost seemed like a day off. When the binder would break, Lynn would simply get down and crawl in the straw until he found the problem. He could not get mad. "It's this here bolt."

Even shaking from drink, he would dive into work without complaint, although he staggered a little when he got to his feet. He had a cunning smile and a squinting eye and he would beckon me with one finger when the other half of something needed picking up.

When we pumped him about the war he said only that he was there. Maybe he'd been married once but she "got away." He had family, but we never got to see them. I don't think he spun tall tales or made brash statements. But always around him, someone was laughing. He used words sparingly, like darts, slipping them in just where they were needed. And each contained a little wisdom, a sharp judgment, because he knew us a lot better than we knew him. He got us. But today I can't remember what those words were. They have blown away like feathers.

He'd work for a couple of weeks, maybe even a month or two, and begin looking nervous.

"Building up, is it?"

"Yeah! Pretty near 't." Just a fact stated with no shame.

Harold by now understood that Lynn's drunkenness wasn't like the sprees of the others. It was more of a natural condition, like frost, so he would make allowances for it. "You can take a couple of days off. But damn it, we need to get that milo off."

And Lynn looked in a hurry for the first time in weeks. He drove off in some old nameless car as faded as he was and disappeared.

A week later, Harold learned he was working for someone else.

This went on for maybe a decade. Lynn became ill, had a leg amputated, and moved to a little trailer in town. His was the only house in Goodland that Harold regularly visited. Mother wanted to know why Harold always went over there.

"He's my friend," Harold said, shaking his head like it was

almost impossible to have such a treasure. A farm can be lonely and all-consuming.

It's funny that I remember Lynn, and not the things he said. He was just like wind on our farm. Gone sometimes but always returning.

Harold carried him into the hospital a few years before the end. Lynn had a lump of constipation in him as big as a football. They saw a pretty nurse. Lynn was slack-faced with pain and said something so low Harold had to bend to hear it. "I hope she works on it," he said.

iron

The Kansas farmer, often an immigrant from the old country, brought with him woodworking and stone-hewing skills. He was a carver and a craftsman. He could cure and tan leathers or tongue-and-groove rough-sawed lumber to make a stock tank. But the Plains were farmed with iron. Even the rheumy-eyed old-timers at the Bird City Threshing Bee have forgotten those old-world crafts. Instead they restore twenties' and thirties' one-cylinder engines or apply green paint to old John Deeres. Plainsmen are metal workers, mechanics, and good shots.

Iron makes tools that wear out slowly and stay sharp and without it the Plains would still be grassland. As you ramble about on old farmsteads, among the fist-sized chunks of foundation rock and finger-sized pieces of crockery scattered by iron implements, a rusted piece of scrap iron pulled from the dirt turns out to be a steel step from a wooden wagon. The wood is long gone, rotted, burned in a stove. With a little brushing off, the buggy step could be bolted to wood and would still be strong enough to support a man.

Steel makes our pistons and gears and plowshares and the frameworks of our machines, but as strong as it is, it constantly breaks or bends and must be mended or returned to shape again. Every farmer is a steel worker and a man who can bend iron never runs entirely out of confidence.

My father stands in the dim shop with the acetylene torch in his hand, adjusting the red knob which controls the acetylene and the green knob which allows the oxygen to flow. When he operates the striker, flint on steel, the torch ignites with a small flaring explosion. This is on our first farm, the one I grew up on. The shop is tin-sided, with high concrete footings and dusty windows over the shop bench on the west side. It is a multipurpose building, joined on the east to a boxcar which serves as a storage room for sacks of feed. The boxcar was lifted on its foundation three feet above the floor before the shop was added on. Inside the shop, a wide concrete lip runs along the front of the boxcar so sacks can be more easily loaded and unloaded from wagons. Below the boxcar is a pit running its length, exuding smells of rotten grain and ancient grease and festooned with the webs and egg sacks of black widow spiders. It is a fearsome hole which I might, in my bravest moments, peer into from the bottom step, but which my father forages in without fear, plunging his hand into dust and webs and crevices amid junk to drag forth what to anyone else would be a forgotten piece of iron.

Harold is obsessed. A thin milo crop needs grinding into ensilage, but the big Bearcat cutter he bought the year before barely strains under its two-row load. It's too slow, so he means to make things more efficient. What he is doing is welding an old McCormick binder to the Bearcat and devising a feeding mechanism so that the feed cut by the binder will pour like a waterfall into the throat of the cutter. The binder cuts six rows at a time, tripling the feeding capacity. He uses the acetylene torch to cut the steel required and the electric welder to put it back together.

He wants me to hold things. I am a portable locking pliers. He gets mad when the sparks fly on me and burn me and I let go. He tells me to get out when he arc welds. The arc is so bright it casts flickering shadows like lightning against the shop walls. If you stare at it long enough you'll burn your eyes. But it is almost impossible not to look in fascination at the tiny blue sun.

He wants a nine-sixteenths, but I can never find them fast enough. When I ask where they are, he always says "over there" or "look on third shelf," when third shelves loom everywhere. I'm proud when I find it.

"About time," he grumps. He's already used the pliers he carries in the pocket of his overalls to wrench the rusted nut free. At school, we have bragging contests about how strong our fathers are.

"My Dad is as strong as a telephone pole."

"My Dad is stronger than a horse."

"My Dad," I say, "is stronger than steel," which ends all argument.

The miscegenation of the binder and the Bearcat gives my father trouble. At supper he complains. "I can't get the feed right."

In his chair, he wrestles with the problem, making gears of his hands and chains of his arms and turning them with his mind. By morning, he has the problem worked out and the sparks fly. He thinks he is a genius when he tows the contraption to the field and it works for a while.

"Now, that's a feed cutter," he says.

It's more complex than that. He's been to Garden City, where a farmer with a welder manufactures low slung green trailers from sheet metal and airplane tires. He bought one. The trailer has a little trough where the rear wheels of the ensilage truck are supposed to rest, so it can be dragged backwards through the field behind the ensilage cutter. This eliminates the truck driver.

Other farmers slow down when they see this incredible complex of machinery being dragged through the field behind the John Deere R. I think some of them will go home and laugh so hard they won't be able to digest their mashed potatoes. A 1930s vintage binder attached to a 1950s Bearcat, with a 1942 R.E.O. truck dragged behind on B-29 tires. "You ought to of seen it."

But it worked, at least for a while, though it always broke down because the hitch wasn't quite right or the feed mechanism Harold had built from scratch wasn't strong enough, but mostly because God had stupid ideas with hard labor.

Stubbornly, he kept at it another year. Now, thirty years later, if you want to look, you can still find the trailer, the Bearcat and the binder in the kochia weed-covered junk pile, although considerable chunks of metal have been sliced off them for other projects.

With enough stock steel, a torch and an electric welder, you can build anything.

If you want to bring a tear to an old farmer's eye, just show him a John Deere D. Despite the binders and threshers, steam tractors and Rumley Oil Pulls, which could run on anything from kerosene to old crankcase oil, Plains farming didn't take its present form until the advent of the John Deere D. With a D, a twelve-foot one-way and a long day, a farmer could turn under forty acres of stubble. Big farmers with lots of children could field platoons of Ds and farm almost anything for next to nothing. Ds were it.

Year after year, the D proved itself in the Nebraska Tractor Tests to be the most economical tractor. That is, you could farm more with less diesel fuel than by any other method. With the D came another invention, the combine. The combine is so called because it is a combination of a McCormick Deering binder and a threshing machine. The first machines were awesome devices, pulled by teams of twelve or more horses. It wasn't long before inventors thought to put an internal combustion engine on the combine, and hook a D to it. Massey Harris started making self-propelled combines. We were on our way.

Since these events occurred, dryland farming hasn't changed much. The tractors and combines have just gotten bigger, as have the farms, while the farmer's families have gotten smaller. And the farmers themselves have become almost as scarce as white-tailed jackrabbits.

Ds or tractors close enough to be called Ds were produced from the late thirties to the fifties. My father still thinks if you have one of those fifties Ds, why you have something. It has to be in good shape, though.

I was born in 1944, when my father was thirty years old. He'd gotten an exemption from military service because he was busy producing food for the world. He made a lot of money then and was busy plowing other fertile fields. My brother had been born three years earlier and my sister would come along about five years later.

Inexorable mathematics meant that by the time I turned eleven and weighed fifty-two pounds, I was ready. I was ripe. My father kept feeling my tiny, stringy biceps with his thumb and forefinger for a reason. Stupid me. I thought it was because he was proud of how strong I was getting. He thumped my head just like he thumped a watermelon to see if it were ripe. He put it in a head lock, to see how much pain I could stand.

And when my fifty-two-pound body had been built up enough by hauling two five-gallon pails of pig slop a furlong to the fence and filling up the water trough with twenty buckets of the same size from the tank an eighth-mile away, he deemed me ready.

1955. I was about to be jerked from my earthworks created by toy trucks and tiny tin tractors in the backyard into the real world of farming. I could be proud then, striding over the land in big boots with my chest stuck out.

He tried me out first when I was ten, on the Oliver 900. The 900 was a wonderful machine, built for pulling heavy loads, but not very versatile. Father used to have two of them. They were wonderful because instead of a single seat like most tractors had, they had a bench seat wide enough for three. In a pinch, the whole family could go for a tractor ride.

My father was stewing, crazy. He had to get something done. Even now I can remember how he was torn between fatherly responsibility (what if I got killed?) and the need to pull rod weeders over 160 acres of ground ahead of the drills. I'd been driving the 900 since I was eight, but never without supervision. He'd let me steer, which went fine until a corner needed turning. The front wheel of the 900 would catch in the one-way furrow and the wheel would spin back out of my control. If I didn't watch it, it would break my thumb. A big hairy forearm would reach over, slamming me back. Slamming me back in disgust — disgust that I just wouldn't grow fast enough to be useful or was so impossibly weak I couldn't wrestle an Oliver 900. He couldn't figure out why I had to be so small when Clark was so large. Hadn't Dr. Richardson, my birth doctor, measured the length at birth of my tibia and predicted I'd be tall?

But by and by, by nine, I'd take the tractor a round by myself, my pectorals straining.

My father couldn't stand it anymore. Labor unused. Labor playing with kittens. Labor dreaming in a bed on an afternoon with a black cat named Nancy. Labor stringing double lengths of garden hose all around the yard and rolling marbles down the crack. Labor chatting happily with its mother at dinner.

"Bruce is coming with me," he told my mother.

"What are you going to do with him?"

"I'm going to put his ass to work."

Who could have been happier? Who could have been prouder?

We drove to that rough quarter southeast of the "other place," fifteen miles from the dinner table, where I stood dwarfed by the Oliver 900.

"Get your ass up there."

I was like a puppy scrabbling over a gate.

Unlike the Rs we had then, the successors of the Ds, the Oliver ran quiet. Then as now, machinery was expensive. What we pulled were two iron-wheeled, thirties-era twelve-foot rod weeders. A rod weeder is simply a frame which holds a turning square rod about an inch in diameter. The rod is pulled just under the surface of the soil. Rod Weeders are still in use. No finer machine has yet been invented to finish summer fallow prior to sowing. He didn't own a proper hitch, though. The weeders trailed behind a sweeps frame with the sweeps removed, one chain longer than the other.

He had that worried look about him. Forty years later, he still gets it whenever he thinks the work is getting behind. We only went a round or two together before he turned me loose. And around and around the field I went, alone, proud, doing a man's work at ten. Every hour or so, he'd come driving over the hill.

I'd stop.

"How you doing?"

I affected a drawl. I stood spraddle-legged in the dirt. I stuck my chest out. I was so stiff with pride I would have fallen except my lace-up farmer's boots wouldn't allow it.

"I guess I'm doing just fine." Nothing to it, Dad. It's easy.

He shook his head. I'll be damned, he seemed to be saying, the way he did when anything worthless turned out to be worth something.

I'd get back on. Away I would go. The pickup would churn back through the dirt, over the hill.

I farmed and farmed, the field got smaller and smaller, the sun got closer and closer to the rim of the earth, and then the field was done. Only the corners were left. I was confident, an earth ripper, striding bigger than life over its face. He'd told me not to, but I wanted him to be proud. I decided to do the corners. What couldn't I do?

Off I went diagonally to the far corner of the field. I spun the wheel around confidently at the end. The tractor responded, turned back toward the center, and then lugged down for some reason. Frantically, I pressed the clutch, but not fast enough. A logchain link whizzed by my head like a thirty-thirty bullet. The tractor died. Behind, the two weeders had snarled together, the paddle wheels pulling them atop the sweeps. I had built a tower of twisted iron twenty feet tall. And I was in big trouble.

I had to walk over the hill. He saw me coming, trudging slump-shouldered, little puffs of dust following my bootheels, and I think he knew what was in store.

"What did you do? Try to do the corners?"

"Yes," I said.

"How bad is it?"

"It isn't too bad. Everything is all piled up is all."

I have never been able to figure out why atheists pray so much. He looked at the sky. "Jesus H. Christ," he said.

That ended tractor-driving that season. Everything worked out in the end. With the scoop tractor, the winch on the Power Wagon and the acetylene torch he and the hired hand got everything straightened out in about a day. I think my father even had a sense of backwards pride in me. No one in his memory had ever screwed up that big. And he admitted in whispers to Mother that I wasn't big enough and the whole deal was really his fault. He may have even told me that on the way home. In farming, if something needs doing, you take risks, even with the lives of small sons.

But why was I never told you could only turn that rig one way?

one way

My reprieve didn't last long. During the next summer, I became a full-fledged farmer. Driving the quiet 900 became a privilege, despite its habit of blowing off the muffler which would land red hot in my lap.

My brother Clark and I drove endless hours pulling oneways behind John Deere Rs. The R was simply a sophisticated D. And also, John Deere's last letter. After the R, Moline (where John Deeres are made) cast away the alphabet in favor of numbers. The new tractors had names like jet airplanes, 4010s and 6030s. The numbers have enlarged almost exponentially, as have the machines.

An R is two Ds, my father said, utilizing curious mathematics. These calculations continue to this day. An 830 was not quite two Rs; the 6030 was almost two 830s, and the 8960 is nearly two 6030s, which means if you really try you can cover 400 acres a day.

A D could pull a oneway over forty acres a day. With an R, I could do eighty. Inexorable mathematics. Farms became twice as big. On the R I quickly learned, after the first week or two, further inexorable mathematics. It takes 202 trips the length of the field to till a quarter section, a distance of 101 miles. At four miles an hour the trip takes twenty-five hours, which meant my brother and I could farm a quarter section in twelve-and-a-half hours, or from sunup to sundown. Dad figured that to be a fair day's work, especially if we were done soon enough to move to the next quarter.

But we didn't go back and forth, because a oneway turned only one way. That's why the machine, a single row of large disks on an angled and weighted frame, was called a oneway. For decades, the oneway was the main tillage implement in dryland farming country. In the fall, I onewayed the wheat stubble to kill the volunteer wheat and weeds and chop up the stubble, around and around. In the spring, Clark and I did it again, and again, maybe three times, before the stubble had been finely enough chopped to "get out the sweeps." Sweeps were large V-shaped blades. Three of them hung on a frame would span twelve feet. The blades travel just under the surface of the soil, which is diverting to watch. They go under a big weed, lift it up, and put it back down were it was, apparently undamaged. On the next pass, the weed is noticeably slumping and by the end of the day it is dried and dead. By early September, the oneways and the sweeps had reduced the soil cover to nothing, which for decades caused the topsoil to blow away when it didn't rain, and to wash away when it did.

The final task before drilling was to rod-weed, great fun, since the weeder pulled light, and a single boy could sometimes farm a whole quarter in a day. Rods, for years, were the machines favored on the Plains to prepare seedbeds.

But sweeps and rod weeders were mere diversions. The oneways were what we spent our summers pulling. It took no brains at all, since we simply followed the furrow left behind by the outer disk of the machine. We went around and around until we reached the center. Then, if we had driven correctly, we went down the diagonal corners, leaving a long furrow, followed by a figure eight turn at the end and another long furrow back to the center of the field. Done properly, it looked almost like an interchange on an interstate highway. Some did it the other way, doubling the furrow in the center, but I always liked the figure eight turn for its symmetry and beauty. If there was slope to the ground, rain would run down these furrows, creating gullies.

At eleven, twelve, thirteen, fourteen, fifteen, sixteen, seventeen, eighteen, nineteen, twenty, twenty-one and twenty-two, I pulled the oneway. All summer, every summer.

The tractors changed a little. The oneways got bigger. We drove John Deere 830s (Eight-Thirties they were called; no one said eight hundred and thirty) and fought over the Forty-ten. The practice continues. Now, my father drives a John Deere Eighty-nine Sixty.

A typical day started with a ride to the field in the pickup. If we were going to the "other place," the land he had bought from Ferd, we'd have a short reprieve. The distance was thirteen miles. In the morning, Harold would usually be in a good mood. He'd be singing, and no matter how cold it was, he'd also have the window open and his arm out.

"Shut the window," we'd cry.

"Oh, are you babies cold?"

But he'd shut it, for thirty seconds. Then he'd freeze us again.

He'd glower at me as I struggled up the tire to pour the five-gallon cans of fuel in the tank. When I began, the cans weighed nearly as much as I did. On lucky days we started from home and filled the machines from gravity-fed tanks. Sometimes we filled from a fifty-gallon drum and a pump that didn't work right. You'd count, for diversion. It took about three hundred strokes to fill the tank. Watching me fill, never fast enough, my father would

tell me I ought to be fucked with a good wood rasp. Many things
needed fucking with a good wood rasp.

When I got done, and was about to get on the tractor, I'd always find he'd been watching. "Did you check the oil?"

Checking oil is a religion. An atheist can get by as long as he
does it. Even if I had checked it, I never did it right. A five-gallon
crankcase a half-pint low was inviting disaster. Filling the fuel
tank was followed by the ritual of greasing. All 1950s machinery
had fittings at every bearing. These were in impossible places.
Machines were always covered with grease, because Harold always made us pump the gun until a healthy gob popped out
along the shafts. "Waste a little grease," was his philosophy.

At last, I climbed over the back of the tractor into the seat,
for John Deere 830s were mounted from the rear. Probably I had
spilled diesel fuel on my pants, and my hands were filthy with
grease. First I turned the gas on to the starter motor, then pushed
the button. It caught. I let it warm for a moment, then reached
down, pulled the decompression lever and the engagement lever,
and the motor turned over. When I released the decompression
lever, the machine began popping, emitting puffs of black smoke.
I opened the throttle and the tractor came to life, running ragged
for a moment and then smoothing out, at least to as smooth as a
two-cylinder John Deere ever got. I switched off the starter engine and shut off the gas and at last was ready to go. It was a
routine as ingrained as cycling. I read in *Esquire* magazine once
about the great bicyclists who trained so intensely they pedaled
in their sleep. In my sleep, thirty-five years later, I still start John
Deeres.

I slid the tractor into second gear and engaged the hand
clutch. You were supposed to do it smoothly, but Dad kept the
clutch adjusted so tight I had to brace myself against the seat and
push it in with my foot. When it caught, the front wheels of the
tractor reared a foot off the ground and then fell back to the field

with a thud. They told us in a 4-H tractor safety class that adjusting a hand clutch too tightly was a good way to get killed, and they showed us photos of legs sticking out from under overturned John Deeres to prove the point. But Harold brushed aside any complaints, even when they came from 250-pound hired hands. He never had any trouble. And besides, if a clutch was loose, you could burn it out. The tractor took the weight of the oneway as I increased the pressure on the hand throttle and I moved out at four miles per hour on my daily journey to nowhere. In many ways, though I was still a child, childhood was over.

school (ha!)

If a medieval inquisitor had been challenged to invent a device to permanently twist children, he would have come up with the one-room school. Ours was District No. 9.

One-room schools were one of the myths my parents and our neighbors eagerly believed in. They should have known of the horrors inside, because they themselves had been miseducated in one-room schools. But they had the attitude that "if it didn't hurt me it won't hurt you." The myth is still perpetuated today, by dozens of *Waltons* episodes and by the few one-room schools that still survive, written about so often in newspapers they are almost as famous as Harvard.

Our parents believed that in them we would learn our ABCs and times tables, the Pledge of Allegiance, and civic responsibilities. The cover of our Kansas history book was etched with fine lines, giving it an almost holographic illusion of motion when moved in light. It was meant to represent the rippling waves of wheat. The school was to our parents like that rippling book, something they couldn't see clearly. Somehow the globe of the world, the copy of the unfinished portrait of George Washington, ink wells and pig tails, floated like clouds of cotton candy in that sentimental world held dear by even the hardest of them. It was here I began to perceive that dichotomy of American philosophy. On one hand is the way things are supposed to be and on the other is how they are.

On our first day of school, we were told to ask if we needed to go to the bathroom. I fell for it the next day.

"Dennis," the teacher said sweetly, "would you help Bruce?"

Dennis was the eighth grader. He'd been shaving for years, and had a body about the shape and consistency of a ham. He leapt to his feet. The old wooden floor sagged a bit in response.

"Yes, Mrs. Truly," he said, the picture of responsibility. She smiled that poodle pucker that animal lovers sometimes have. Her head, too, was filled with one-room-school cotton candy. The big kids could help the little kids. That's what made country schools special.

We did our business outside, in outhouses. The teacher could see Dennis, his hand on mine, leading me to the toilet. "Look how Dennis is taking on responsibility," she may have said to herself in self-congratulation.

Once inside the outhouse, Dennis pinned my neck to the wall and with his other hand he reached inside my pants and pinched my penis between his thumb and forefinger, squeezing it so hard I nearly puked. Then he pulled it, like a coyote unreeling a gut, and let it snap back. He repeated this procedure several times.

"From now on, you hold it," he said. Then he got out his pocket knife and told me what would happen if I ever told.

Ah, education, how quickly one can learn in a one-room school. But District No. 9 had a problem. Little kids were constantly peeing their pants. It was even discussed at school board meetings. Our parents figured we'd grow out of it, which we did eventually.

Who could blame our parents for sentimentalizing the one-room school? What could be more homey? How could we have been safer, only a few miles from home? What could have been handier, when hands were needed for work? What could have looked more peaceful, with the coal smoke drifting in winter from the stovepipe?

Our school was located three miles from my home, on its own five-acre patch of buffalo grass populated by ground squirrels. Dennis trapped mice, and put them atop a layer of dirt in the metal waste can. Then he caught a ground squirrel, which we tamed in class to the point it would crawl up our pants legs. Dennis wanted to know what would happen if he put the ground squirrel in the mouse pen.

The ground squirrel killed the mice one by one and skinned them. The last mouse survived for a time by hiding under a jar lid used for water. Dennis flipped the lid over. After the ground squirrel killed the final survivor, Dennis caught the squirrel, took it outside and chopped it in half with an ax. Then he burned the body with the kerosene used to light the stove. This is how we learned about biology.

The school was rectangular and plain, its only appliance a coal stove which stood next to the teacher's desk. Our desks were the old-fashioned kind, fastened in rows on wooden rails and still equipped with ink wells, though wise teachers preferred pencils. The building was entered through a small hall, where coats were hung, lunch pails stowed and a five-gallon crockery jug kept. Outside were the two outhouses, one for each sex, and a horse barn filled with prairie hay.

The school's books were kept in a single green upright locker, and were mostly outdated textbooks and a 1920's version of the *Book of Knowledge,* a whole chapter of which was devoted to "match manufacture." But the encyclopedias also contained color plates, faded with time, of "Butterflies of the World," and "Creatures of the Deep Sea." I was bug-eyed.

Once my toilet training was completed, the early weeks passed quickly. Dennis continued to size me up, ever willing to further my education. Though I did not know it, that first year was not only a struggle for survival, but also a choice between good and evil. Good was the half-finished portrait of George Washington, the Pledge of Allegiance, and informing on the eighth-graders in time to prevent them from immolating a captured ground squirrel in kerosene. Evil was the attitude of eighth-graders and imitating them as they said, "I pledge my 'legiance to the old hag of the blackboard slates and the cunt tree on which she stands, one nation invisible, with freedom and just us for all."

I desperately wanted to earn the praise of my teacher, yet I longed for the respect of Dennis Smith, who was our leader. To this end, I swung higher and higher on the homemade swings, bailing out at more and more precipitous angles, yelling "Look at me, look at me," as I flew through the air.

These were no ordinary swings. Built by our fathers from rural electrification poles, they dwarfed the swings in the city playgrounds. The swing seat dangled from thirty feet of chain. With proper effort one could reach a height of over twenty feet and with a well-timed bailout could catapult a lateral distance of fifty feet. But though I swung higher and bailed further than any first-grader in the history of District No. 9, Smith ignored me.

The swings produced several broken ankles each year, but the merry-go-round was even more dangerous. This was also a homemade device based on an axle and wheel salvaged from an old threshing machine. The axle was buried upright in concrete; heavy angle iron was welded to the old wheel to make a platform for the seats, which were made of splintery bridge planks. Altogether, the device must have weighed a ton. The idea was for several children to run inside the wheel, pushing the contraption to fantastic speeds, while the smaller children riding on the outside screamed in fear before being thrown by centrifugal force into a six-foot deep grader ditch full of thistles.

Being flung into the grader ditch was the best possible out-
come of riding the merry-go-round. Far worse was falling under
it, to be scalped by the angle irons as they passed overhead, the
noggin acting like the safety device in a ratcheted windlass.

This frequent accident created head wounds messy enough
that the teacher was forced to drive the half-mile to the nearest
farm house to phone for help. By the time the parents arrived the
student's face, hair, and shirt would be coated with blood, which
conferred a certain status, if temporary. The party lines would be
busy that night.

"How many stitches?" anxious grandmothers would ask.

Ten was average; the record was twenty-six.

Our progress through District No. 9 was measured by
knuckles nicked by teacher's rulers and dented heads.

Though I did not realize it, the war within me between
good and evil was about to be decided, not by my choice, but
through force. I was about to fall forever out of the favor of the
teacher due to a diabolical plot. Dennis Smith engineered my
disgrace.

In the third month of the first grade, having been properly
toilet trained, I was taken into his confidence.

"Good jump," he would say as I bailed from the swing.

"Nice catch," he would yell encouragingly, as his bat pro-
pelled a softball into my midriff, where it stuck. I reveled in every
word of praise, suspecting nothing.

I came to worship him. One day he asked me if I really liked
Beverly Pancake. Beverly was a wondrous slender creature of yellow curls, budding curves, and instinctual maternity who smiled
at me each morning as I, the only first-grader and the tiniest of
all the students, took my seat.

"Yes," I said innocently. "She's nice."

"Then tell her a secret," he said. "Tell her this, but remember
it's a secret, so whisper."

He told me what to say. I thought it was a secret code. I approached Beverly timorously.

"Dennis told me to tell you a secret," I said.

"Well, what is it?" she asked. She was stuck on him.

"I'll have to whisper," I said.

She bent her ear to my lips, her blond curls tickling my face. I repeated the words I had been told. Then I was lying on the floor, half dazed, wondering if the wet fluid coming from my ears was blood.

Mrs. Truly descended like a lioness. "What did that child say?" she asked.

Beverly blushed in embarrassment. "I can't say, it's too dirty."

They disappeared into the hall. I had recovered enough to crawl back into my seat, still crying in fear and pain while the big kids sniggered. I began to realize I had been betrayed. Mrs. Truly stomped back into the room from the hall.

"You little sex fiend," she snorted in disgust, and I was back on the floor again, my face stinging from a second slap. At home I got no sympathy. Mother's opinion was that a child with a mouth that filthy should have it washed with Lava soap.

"But I didn't know," I protested.

"You did too," she said, with the assurance of generations of women.

I had been branded bad. Evil had won. I couldn't after that moment become good even if I had wanted to. Two months later, we were watching Dennis fucking Eleanor Darby behind the hay barn along with other boys.

I knew he wasn't supposed to be fucking Eleanor behind the hay barn. When Dennis was done, having pumped out a healthy load, it was our turn. To ensure compliance in the crime, Dennis decided we'd all have to participate. So, one by one, we were led up to her, to press our soft pee pees against her hairless slit, while Eleanor grinned. Poor Eleanor, she was just a homely girl who wanted to be popular. And she was very popular, with the fifth grade on up.

We did what Dennis said and were proud. We felt grown up, having heard all our lives the secret whisperings of our parents about the mysterious act of "fucking." A whole new world. Dennis had us in the palm of his hand, so to speak. We did what he said.

Somehow though, word of our extracurricular activities leaked out. Sex always leaks out, no matter how clandestine. All of the children were questioned closely, especially me, as I was already a documented sex fiend. Of course, my brother was never a suspect. He already had the reputation of seriousness, and religious, monk-like pursuit of his studies. He had a pair of haunches on him, though, as I had observed behind the barn.

The school board took drastic action. They hired a man.

By the time I faced this new teacher I was in the second grade and Dennis had escaped into high school, where he had been drafted into the interior line of the football team the day he showed up on the front step in his bib overalls. Who says crimes are always punished? In high school he became a hero and one of the most legendary cocksmen ever produced by Sherman County.

Our new teacher was proof that nothing ever changes — he simply replaced Dennis as head bully. He used the simplest of methods. He chose his favorites, who were allowed to get away with anything, and he picked on the rest of us. His teaching method toward us unfavored was to beat us until we got it right. He used a large paddle while forcing us to hold our ankles. I could not stand up to these, and always broke into tears. Thus, I was chosen as the one to be beaten most often.

It's all a blur now. Somehow, I learned to read with speed and accuracy, but never out loud without stuttering. That thick paddle still hovers over me. I read through the Carnegie Public

Library, through the Science Fiction Book-of-the-Month Club. I got into mother's Frank Yerby novels and crawled up in the attic and found *Forever Amber*. I read it, and then I read it again. And when I read, I escaped. I read on the rooftop of the chicken house, I read under the covers with a flashlight long after being told to go to sleep, I read in closets, just because it struck my fancy, and high in the branches of trees in a military poncho fashioned into a hammock.

When the state legislature decreed that the tiny school districts were to be consolidated into larger ones and the position of county school superintendent abolished, our parents fought it with their last bitter breath. The aftertaste of the battle still lingers over rural Kansas, but the consolidations continue inexorably. The population shifts from rural areas to small towns, the small towns dry up and the schools close. Every district desperately fights for every student it can find.

I attended seventh grade in Goodland. I was the kid who lived at the end of the bus route. The school was a squat and ugly building, three tiers of dark brick cut with tiny black windows. The school day began with gym class. I stood in my white shorts, a five-foot-tall, sixty-two-pound seventh grader. The gym teacher asked if there were any of us who didn't know how to play basketball.

Timorously, I raised my hand.

He grabbed me by the ear and dragged me about the court. "This is the baseline," he said, pointing downward, "and that is the goal," he said, pointing upward, while the lines of gym-clad, all knowing town kids tittered. By then I was well on my way to understanding education.

the pool

I think now that my father felt guilty about the way he worked us. But he balanced that guilt against his own needs. He was building a farm, and my brother and I were cheap labor. He may have even calculated it out on a pad. No way he could pay men to run those two tractors and make those payments. But I also think he checked us like he did the oil and when our crankcases filled with gunk and tiredness, he serviced us as deliberately as he did his machines. He let us go to the pool! Such occasions would come like an unexpected Christmas.

"You boys get that quarter done, and your mom will take you in swimming."

It's an example of how, when you are not jaded, it takes very little to make you happy. Here was a chance for mindless escape from responsibility. Floating, goofing off.

Kansas has always been a place for swimming pool mania. The world's largest swimming pool (so they claim) is in Garden City. Colby was proud of its pool, too. I can't remember its dimensions, but it contained about a billion cubic feet of water, or so it was advertised on Kay Triple X, and traitorously on

Goodland's own KWGB (Kansas Women Grow Big). The two towns had been fighting for decades, trying to decide which would wind up as the regional economic center. Colby eventually won, though Goodland doesn't know it yet. Then, even tiny St. Francis, a heat-soaked, tree-choked hole in a valley, had a swimming pool, and advertised it. Any town worth anything had a pool.

Western Kansans will regularly turn down school bond issues, even when the school is falling down. But almost every time they'll vote for a pool, no matter how much it costs. The wives see to it.

I know enough about my hometown to know that the city council didn't get teary-eyed over tiny panting children when they finally sprang for the Goodland pool. It was probably business as usual which inspired them finally to build the finest swimming pool between Kansas City and Denver. Main Street wanted those harassed mothers who increasingly drove to St. Francis and Colby and left their little buggers at the pool. What better way to stop this treacherous leakage of business than to build the world's largest glass-enclosed swimming pool? Heated, too, unlike Colby's, where the water pumped straight out of the Ogallala aquifer was cold enough to freeze your tush.

So the airwaves were filled with bombast, and Goodland stuck its chest out proud, and the local paper, the *Goodland Daily News,* printed pictures of splay-legged teenagers in midair and captioned these "high dive."

"Glass-enclosed" was a slight misnomer; it meant only that the fence was built of large glass sheets reinforced with chicken wire. These panels intercepted parental shouts, forcing the parents to go inside to fetch us. Whenever a parent approached the edge of the pool, waves of water would erupt, soaking them.

The pool was something. It was 120 feet long and 60 feet wide and sported three diving boards. It was a pee-filled paradise. My brother and I stayed in until we were shriveled like un-cured hides.

As far as my father was concerned, we were being "given a good swim." But other things were also happening. The pool was the only place where we might encounter that strange species, the town kid. From them, we quickly learned we were back-wards. We learned at the pool that there was life outside of driving a tractor. Town kids swam every day. They were given quarters and lolled about downtown, living like pashas. They played baseball in summer leagues, and by the sixth grade had girlfriends. Their fathers did not work on Sundays, or even Saturdays. It was a lackadaisical life. It was called being a child.

I was filled with unspeakable admiration for this life. Sodas, swimming, games, indoor dogs, and, most of all, friends. Town kids had friends. My world, in comparison, was tiny, truncated, and because of the wondrous pool, I knew it.

How my brother Clark and I related to this vast new world of town kids is a key to our personalities. My brother was stead-fast, observed the rules, and did not believe little kids were merely fair game to be splashed, dunked, and drowned. He would not do that stuff, except to me. I so desperately wanted my new friends' approval, I would do anything. Any dare was im-mediately taken. I'd jump off the high board in any position. I learned back flips and front flips. I provoked the lady lifeguards, who were as mean and snappy as weasels, and blew their whistles at me so hard their eyes popped. I acquired friends.

Clark was more timid, less flexible. Even then, his sense of right and wrong was cast in concrete, which caused him too often to expose his prognathous jaw, a habit which often in his life would get it popped. He fought one night like a lion to pro-tect strangers who were traveling through town, while I was on the side of the town kids who were persecuting them. They were so grateful they sent my brother Christmas cards for years afterwards, which he took as proof of the rewards of being good. Of course I tried to glom on to his glory, claiming I would have protected them too, if only I had known what was going on. "But you were on the other side," my brother pointed out.

These differences persisted into our adult life. Until he died, my brother loved to swim, and I still do. My wife got me one of those lawn chairs supported in the water by Styrofoam. Sometimes I roll off it and float, maybe even swim a stroke or two if I'm in the mood. My brother swam in triathlons.

julene

Riding back with us from the swimming pool, probably next to Mother in the favored front seat, was my sister Julene. No doubt she was basking in my disfavor, her little face upturned, ignoring me. She knew how to pile it on when I was down.

Her arrival, perhaps seven years before, when I was five, had both disadvantages and advantages. I was no longer cute. My jokes didn't work anymore. I was discovering what millions of middle children before me had discovered — that as soon as a new baby is born the one before is simply abandoned. The advantage was that parental supervision, except when I was caught misbehaving, was over. If I put on my snowsuit and escaped into a blizzard, no one gave a damn. When I came home from forays in the pastures, scared to the center by encounters with rattlesnakes, my pockets filled with shiny pebbles, dead insects, seeds, and rodent skulls, and brought forth these treasures to show Mother, I was told to get out of the kitchen. Mother was busy brushing Julene's hair.

Both Clark and I were fascinated with her at first. She was a cute thing, cooing in her cradle.

"Get away from there," Mother would scream.

It was as if girl children were the most fragile of creatures in nature, as delicate as milkweed silk. Our very breath might destroy her. I quickly found out this was not so, giving her a few stiff pokes on occasion just to see what would happen. These elicited the most amazing squalls.

Later we played together, me chasing her through the house, while she, a chubby creature of golden curls, squealed in mock fear. But when I tired of the game and retreated to my room to contemplate my cigar boxes filled with biological specimens, she would fake injury at my hands to get even. And no matter how preposterous the lie, she was always believed. When I was punished for whatever it was that I hadn't done to her, I had to endure the double humiliation of seeing her peering around the corner, enjoying her revenge. These encounters taught me a valuable lesson. Julene was a person to stay away from.

But staying away wasn't easy. I knew every nook and hiding place on the farm, but soon she did too. I could climb atop impossibly precipitous farm buildings, hoping she would follow and die. Of course, she would only fall a little way, and I would be punished because I hadn't stopped her. "You're supposed to look after your little sister."

I could have bumped her off if my parents hadn't filled in the ensilage pit in the horse barn. This was a round hole, twenty feet across and forty feet deep, dug years before by Grandfather Carlson. My brother and I would crawl out on the rafters above it. I learned to climb young, as a way of escaping Clark when he was mad at me, and my ultimate refuge was to hang by my hands over the empty pit.

"Come on and get me."

Clark would cautiously edge out on the rafters, making sure to always have a handhold.

"Ha, scared, aren't you," I would yell, and swinging, I could completely release myself over the pit and catch hold of the next rafter two feet away. "Betcha can't do that."

But as soon as my sister was old enough to walk, my parents had the pit filled because Julene might fall in.

This period of sibling struggle lasted only a few years. The John Deere took care of most of it, and school most of the rest. But I had to watch her still. Once, on Main Street, she shut my fingers in the car door. It took Mother a full minute to comprehend what had happened. I was screaming so loud cars came to a stop. At last, released, I bent over my hand, holding it, crying, examining the torn fingernails and the blood.

"Oh, I didn't mean it. Oh, I didn't mean it," Julene said. She was crying almost as loud as I was. Mother was so distraught she took Julene in her arms. "There, there," she said. "I know you didn't." But I saw Julene's face, peering over Mother's shoulder and that quick, supercilious smirk of triumph that was so characteristic of her and I knew she had done it on purpose.

My parents really believed girls were sugar and spice and everything nice. Julene had the best room, with windows on each side so it would be cool. It was also the nearest to my parents' room, so that if she might cough in the night she could be succored. She slept in a queen-sized bed. Her dresser tops were crammed with perfumes and statuary of horses. She begged to be given a real one, but here caution prevailed until she was perhaps ten. At last Harold gave in.

"There's something about girls and horses that go together," my father declared. The first was Queenie, a brown mare. My sister, already convinced she was an accomplished horsewoman, eagerly clambered aboard, to be led about at first, then bellowed when soloing because Queenie would not do what she wanted. Harold declared that Queenie had to be ridden down by a man, and chose me for the task.

Years before, I had jumped from the rafters onto the back of an unbroken colt, one of the progeny of work horses which simply existed without care on our farm. They were huge spotted animals, with unkempt and split hooves the size of dinner plates. The horse immediately bolted but somehow I stayed on. My brother gave chase in the pickup, and I saved myself from a fall by leaping into the back. We had kept this to ourselves.

I hadn't learned a thing. I jumped on Queenie and whipped her to full gallop. We went through the farmyard and into the windbreak, where Queenie ran for the nearest overhanging branch. Lying there with the wind knocked out of me I looked up to see Queenie looking back, regarding me through a bulbous horse eye and with an expression of supercilious superiority. I didn't want to get back on her, but I did. Manhood, duty, and dignity demanded it. And I nearly rode that mare to death, returning her to Julene in a lather.

"That's what it takes," my father said.

"Oh, poor Queenie," my sister moaned.

She did become a good rider, slender and erect in the saddle, her ponytail flying. As Clark and I circled the fields endlessly on the John Deeres, the pickup towing the horse trailer would pass. Dressed in the red and fringed regalia of the Prairie Pioneers Riding Club, she did not even pretend to notice us. And we would choke on the dust.

vacations

Our world was not totally truncated. In our early years we took a vacation every year, though I was so small I can barely remember them and Julene was only a baby. We got all the way to California once — pretty far for Bairs.

I was about eight. Clark and Harold went out on a deep sea fishing boat, and Clark came back proudly with six red snappers. Harold had caught nothing. He had become seasick. What else would you expect from a flatland farmer?

We ate at one of those cafes on the wharf which specialized in cleaning and cooking the catches of charter boat clients. I refused to eat the fish, I was so jealous. This time was so long ago the big gasoline trucks crossing the mountains dragged log chains behind them on the asphalt, producing trails of sparks. The trucks were the source of an old family legend. Someone had told mother that semis burned corn cobs and she believed it, probably because of the old phrase, "pouring the cobs to it."

On one of these trips, while traveling behind a big truck smoking up a mountain, Mother told us that the sleeper was where they kept all the corn cobs.

"What?" said Harold. He was already grinning.

"That's where they keep the corn cobs they burn."

Dad started roaring with laughter, and Mother got madder and madder and sat straighter and straighter in her seat, her arms locked across her breasts.

"You don't really think they burn corn cobs, do you?" asked Harold.

Mother was rigid now. It all went back to her upbringing. How in high school she had felt so out of it, just a klutz from the country. Her teen years were probably even more awkward than our own. Her parents were from the old country. And how many times had she been humiliated by innocently expressing some ignorant superstition passed down through her family? And now it was happening to her again, in front of her own family.

So for years afterwards, whenever we wanted to get her, we mimicked her in that Carlson drawl, "How many corn cobs you suppose it's burning?"

This trip to California cost the princely sum of four hundred dollars, and Harold would pull his stash out of his billfold at times to show us. We were true Bairs even by then. Nothing made our eyes grow larger than a hundred dollar bill.

But I think the trip to California was the last real trip, the last time we ever went anywhere together as a family except to Denver. Something changed.

Harold was in a hurry to swath, and did not bother bolting the power takeoff shield between the machine and the old row crop Minneapolis. He had done that before, though it meant at times straddling the shaft as he drove. But this time the shaft grabbed his overall, whipped the cloth away, and began tearing at his flesh. He was lucky in one respect. He managed to shut the shaft down with a last grasp. If he hadn't, the machine would have probably wrapped him up and spewed him out in pieces. As it was, it got only a large part of his calf. He looked down with no particular horror. Tendons were exposed, and the large chunk of flesh that was his calf muscle flapped on a hinge of tissue. He has told us this story many times, usually with instruction to always install the shields.

"I didn't think it was so bad," he said. "I could get around with one foot."

He found he could walk by standing on the toe of his wounded leg, and struggled to the road. Someone passing by found him. By this time he had nearly bled to death. They used a belt for a tourniquet and that slowed the bleeding some. He was half alive when he got to the hospital in Goodland.

I remember that while Harold was in the hospital we were shuffled around to Grandma Bair's and Aunt Irene's. The family pitched in to allow Mother to make daily trips to the hospital. Leonard Bashford took his vacation and drove from Lupton, Colorado in his old black Dodge. He sowed our wheat and saved our farm. What he planted grew into a bumper crop.

The wounds were bad, but not permanent. The doctors sewed Harold's calf back on, and patched over the wound with tissue from his thigh. It didn't look very good, but it worked. Then Dr. Laslie decided that more reconstructive surgery would have to be done. They put my father's legs together in a cast, the idea being for them to grow together. After several weeks, they were to be sliced apart again, one leg contributing flesh to the other.

It was during this period that my father entered a world of pain, his strongest memory if you can judge memories by what people talk about. He did things that he never dreamed he could sink to doing. He begged for morphine. But the physicians and nurses wouldn't give him enough of it. So he yelled, and screamed and cursed for it. All of this he now relates to me, shaking his head at the memory.

"I suppose if I could have I would have taken a gun and blown my brains out."

And this is from a man who has beaten a stroke and, at eighty, thinks congestive heart failure is just another little setback to be overcome. The pain must have been horrible.

He fooled us children. We were taken to see him, and he just lay there grinning without complaint. It was an act. Usually, when we wanted to see him we were told we couldn't.

When he was released from his hospital bed after six weeks, he was like a lion freed. He'd race across the floor on his crutches, though at this time Mother was still changing bandages over suppurating flesh. And once, when a hired hand drove the truck away from the gasoline tank, pulling the hose free, Harold raced on crutches all the way across the farmyard, and somehow got a barrel under the stream of gasoline and climbed atop it and pounded a corncob in the hole to save the gas, even though his bandages got soaked.

I was a witness to that incident, and he was in a rage at me for not knowing what to do. Or if I did know, not doing it because I did not want to be soaked with gasoline. And that is the way he remained for years afterwards. The pain had done something to him. It had wiped out the remnants of his youth, although he was still young, and had turned him serious. At the time, I had a lump of sorry sympathy in my throat for my father's hurt, but I couldn't get over my own sorrow at what amounted to losing my Dad. We had no more of those nights lying on the ground together while he misnamed the constellations. He'd gotten through the pain by employing a great rage, and as with all great emotions, it changed him.

It was afterwards that the trips stopped, and the good times were over. No, these times were not bad, either. They were just busy. We marched forth and built the farm. After my father's injury, no time was left for fun.

childhood friends

Before I became a tractor driver, I played by myself ninety percent of the time. We had neighbor children, and I was sometimes carted over to play with them, or I walked the two or three miles or rode a bicycle.

It helped alleviate the loneliness of living isolated from other children, but not much. I had only two friends. One was Marvin Seaman, whose dad had been in the Navy. The other was Darrel Pettijohn. Being friends with Darrel was like being a friend of a mean rooster. He was incapable of playing cooperatively. You'd spend all day building a dirt castle, and at the end of the day he would kick it over. He liked to catch bull snakes and lay them over electric fences. He told me he had drilled a hole in a cat's tail and threaded the electric fence through the hole.

"The cat didn't do anything when I drilled the hole, but you should have heard him howl when I turned on the fence."

Since he was determined to be a hellcat, his grandmother, my Aunt Irene, equipped him with boxing gloves. He used these to ceaselessly pummel his younger brother, Mark. When Darrel and I got into it, we were separated and put into the basement, told to don the gloves, and go to it. These fights were refereed by adults, who surrounded us like spectators in a pitbull ring. Since he worked as hard as I did, he was just as strong and he was tougher than me, and wiry, and usually could whip me, just because he was meaner. He used a combination of punching speed and groin kicks. But provoked past tears and into rage, I was more than his match, and when I managed to land a telling blow, he'd bawl and run to his grandmother. But even then, I learned, I couldn't drop my guard. He'd sucker punch me in the back of the head as I walked up the stairs. If I protested, Aunt Irene would say, "You only got what was coming to you."

Marvin and I were best friends for years. We attended the same school, and learned its lessons well. One of our games was initiating his younger brother Brian into our club. We accomplished this by tying him to a post, pulling his penis, and leaving him there for hours.

But our parents let us know in hundreds of ways, even though we often ate dinners together, that the Seamans were our social inferiors. For one thing, their mother Opal sewed their shirts, which made them look funny somehow. Our clothes were store-bought at Penny's. The Seamans were even more homespun than we were, and tighter, if that could be imagined, with a dollar. My mother couldn't get over how tiny their sugar spoon was. Even then, we were on our way to being well off, while the Seamans resisted progress. Bill, Marvin's dad, wasted time with photography and hunted arrowheads instead of being a real farmer.

"They just set out on that little place and don't do anything," sneered my father.

But Bill Seaman's interests were wider than my father's and he possessed treasures of industry unsuspected by him. One was the huge cache of photographs of nude women in the darkroom and a complete set of *Sunset,* a nudist magazine. One shot of a young woman standing on one foot, the other behind her head, particularly impressed me. And upstairs, on the wall, were hundreds of arrowheads in frames. Bill knew which tribe had made every one. His greatest find was an obsidian eagle, which occupied the central spot in the central frame.

Tired of these treasures, Marvin and I would retire to the huge barn, always half filled with hay. Bill had strung a rope from the rafters. You could swing on it like Tarzan, clear across the mow. Marvin and I took turns, though we'd been warned a thousand times not to do it. We made dares, to see who could do the most dangerous tricks, knocking our wind out in the process. And I believe it was a standoff. But always between Marvin and me was that unspoken feeling of our family's superiority. When we bragged, I could brag about what really mattered in western Kansas, the land we owned, the tractors we drove, the money we made. We were on our way to becoming rich and they were merely making do. When at last I entered public school in Goodland, I abandoned Marvin, who had up to then been my best friend. His homespun shirts and homespun ways made him even more vulnerable than me, as I fiercely fought to join the cliques.

Today, what I went through might be called a "lack of socialization." By the time my brother and I were at last released from the country school, and later from bondage on the farm, it was too late for us. In the high school social whirl we were like puppies raised without siblings. We didn't know how to act, our place in the pecking order hadn't been established, we hadn't grown up and gone to school with the other children, and so were always outsiders.

My efforts to become one of the group were pathetic. My name was never mentioned in the high school newspaper, my picture never taken, except as necessary for the yearbook. My brother used morality to outdo them all. He studied, he stuck up for what was right, and became valedictorian. My sister was a hybrid. She got some town life, and I think did better at it than the two of us. Clark and I were "backwards sons-a-bitches," as my father called us after overhearing our thousandth unsuccessful attempt to get a date. But being backwards was no more than self-reliance, and in the end it turned out to be good for us.

discipline

I like to think sometimes of hawks hovering over us, looking down on our red-roofed house. Thinking of them, I can still
whirl down through the air and the roof and into the bedroom
where Clark and I slept. He was a smelly-footed creature and
difficult to sleep with. He hugged me in the night, a practice that
became much more desperate as he grew older. And when I had
the nightmare about the panther that could pull itself into its
own head and chase me like a rolling ball, he was unsympathetic.
"Shut up and go back to sleep, you little pissant."

We were often enemies, but sometimes stood up for one another. Never were we closer than that night Harold roared into
our room and began fiercely beating Clark.

What was unusual about it was the intensity. Common beatings were normal. Hardly any family on the Plains was above
giving a child a good beating, although they couldn't talk about
it without euphemism. Our parents discussed it too, scoffing in
mirth at the theories of Dr. Spock, who held that children
shouldn't be "spanked." Spank was their euphemism for what
they did to us.

This debate was of great interest to children, also. We soberly discussed this subject at school. We were especially interested in technique. Some dads used boards, some used their hand, and others a belt. Ours used a belt, a symbol of terror fetched from the upstairs closet with ritual.

The ritual began when Mom would tell us that when Dad came home we were going to get it. Most of the time she got over whatever had caused her anger, often something Julene told her we had done. But sometimes she didn't. We could never tell which it would be. The same offense that one day might produce an indulgent chuckle could on another so provoke her that when Harold came home, she would meet him tight-lipped in the kitchen.

We weren't supposed to listen. Being caught listening at the door was an offense. We weren't supposed to overhear any of our parents' secret conversations. It was sneaky and being sneaky was one of the worst offenses. But not knowing was almost worse than the punishment. So we listened at the door, caught voice clues and scurried away at the sound of approaching footfalls. Our parents were tricky, though, sometimes sneaking around from the other direction. And often, these beatings might be carried out with high good humor, as if our parents were enjoying our terror.

Inside the kitchen, Harold might say loudly, "Ah, Jasmin." This meant we would get no punishment. It was naturally understood that women sometimes over-reacted to what were merely childhood pranks. But most likely, we were doomed.

"I'm going to get the belt," he would say, striding through the kitchen door. Boom, boom, boom, up the stairs. Boom, boom, boom, through the hall and into the bedroom. A quieter moment followed, as he rustled in the closet. And then the return . . . boom, boom, boom, footsteps of doom causing the floor to shake.

Absolutely no childish stratagem could save us now. Running out the door wouldn't work. Mother would come out every thirty minutes and stand on the steps while we whimpered in the weeds, getting hungrier and hungrier. "You're just going to make it worse."

And we'd try to weasel deals about how many swats the offense was worth. But she would only say with great satisfaction, "In fact, you've already made it worse."

Crawling under the bed was no defense. Even if I curled in the darkest corner, with knees pulled to chest, Harold could reach his arm under and drag me out like a hedgehog as I frantically clung to the bed legs. I was the one who hid in the weeds and clung to the bed legs. My brother had already learned the uselessness of such tactics, or perhaps he had never used them. He bore most affronts with stoicism. In fact, it seems to me now that I was inordinately punished in comparison with Clark.

Clark always figured if he were to be beaten, his pain could be lessened if he could implicate me. This seemed to work well for him, but when I tried it, I usually got six extra swats for lying. "Clark wouldn't do that," Mom would say. "Only you would do that."

And she was usually right.

Harold didn't use the "bend over and grab" method. He'd pin us down with one hand, or hold us up by the overall straps, sometimes upside down, and somehow give us six or seven stinging swats, which left red marks and sometimes welts.

But the night he invaded our room, he outdid himself. I think I said, "What the hell's it for?" Which caused him to promptly start beating me, too. He hit us so hard that we turned over, trying to ward away the blows with our hands. We burrowed under the covers and tried to get away, but he got us by the foot.

"What's it for? What's it for?" my brother kept crying. The truth of spanking is that it is not the tragedy our New Age child psychologists claim it to be, so long as it is consistent. You do something bad, and you know the risk — the punishment is fair. You does the crime, you does the time. But it can wound deeply and instill distrust for months when it is unfair. It was important to know why, so we would not risk it again, or at least, could be more sneaky the next time. But Harold that night wouldn't tell us. "You know what it's for," he said when he was done, looking down at us in utter disgust. He slammed our door like it was hinged to a dungeon wall.

We cried a long time. The average beating only produced a minute's tears. We were bruised from ankles to mid-back but we were alive.

"What was that for?" I asked.

"I don't know," said Clark. His fists were balled, and he was tight with rage.

I still don't know what it was for. Maybe it had something to do with sex.

sex

I don't know why our parents got so excited about the subject of sex. Sex was everywhere. When the stallion was brought out to "service" Queenie, it was an event for the whole family to watch. The stallion's dork was reeled out like a radiator hose two minutes after he was in the corral.

Sex then commenced, starting with the pair running around the corral, kicking up their heels and farting. It took an hour or two for the consummation. The stallion was all bunched up and looked like he might die. Queenie contentedly chewed hay. (It isn't much different with humans, I later learned.)

After getting a good look at what was happening in the corral, Mother would stomp off, usually muttering something about filth. She was a Lutheran, and couldn't help it. And dinner would be constrained because it really wasn't polite to talk about the most interesting happening of the day.

Out in the pastures, when the forty or fifty rams were turned in, whole herds of animals fucked. We observed this in detail as part of our training in husbandry. A ram cock was a curved and pointed affair, which took about three humps to get off. When they weren't fucking, the rams smelled ass. And in certain seasons, when nature seemed not to cooperate, Harold would worry and say, "There's not enough fucking going on."

Of course, there always was and always will be.

By the age of six, we had a good idea of what was going on, though the connection between animals and humans remained fuzzy. By that age, and well into high school, all of our stumbling analogies were of animals. Things hunched like sheep, barked like dogs, rooted and snorfled like hogs, and fucked like stallions. So why were our parents so shocked when we tried to imitate them? During family gatherings my brother and I and our male cousins had ample opportunity to sneak off into the weeds with our female cousins. There, purely in the interests of anatomical study, we would barter.

"If you take off your panties, I'll take off my underwear." We would then observe the apparatus. And if, in the interest of the expansion of knowledge, one of the larger of us may have lain face and dungarees down amid pantyless thighs, as the rest squatted in the weeds watching, so what? I can tell you now with the keen eye of a husbandryman, no penetration ever occurred.

Our behavior prior to these occurrences partially gave us away. We'd twitter in the corner with blankets over our heads.

"What are we gonna do?"

He-he, he-he, twitter-twitter.

"Let's tell dirty stories."

"No, if we're going to tell dirty stories, I'm leaving." You could see the pure face of the righteous girl, uptilted, seeking the light of God, even in the dimness under the sheets.

"Spoilsport, nincompoop, pantywaist," and the ultimate insult, "chicken."

This would quickly break her down, and then she would play the game all the way out into the weeds with as much enthusiasm and interest as any of the rest of us.

Here is one of our stories.

A young black boy is eating watermelon on a sidewalk. As he eats, he slaps at flies.

"Goddamned flies," he yells, just as a priest walks by.

"Son, son, son," says the priest, "God has use for everything. Just name me three useless things."

"Tits on a nun, pecker on a priest, and these goddamned flies," says the boy.

We snuffled and squirmed and giggled under the blankets like dirty maggots, we were so happy. Inevitably, a parent with a long memory would check our corner.

"WHAT'S GOING ON UNDER THERE? YOU STOP THAT. GET OUT OF HERE, GET OUT OF THIS HOUSE."

Children playing in the sun were certainly more healthful. And we'd head straight for the weeds. It got so quiet. The sun was down. What was going on out there? Where had we been? They saw in our stances, even Clark's, that something unsavory had transpired. They would sniff the air. It was sex and they knew it.

At last the wronged and righteous girl would, while being held by the arm by her mother as the other adults ringed around, tearfully confess, pointing her finger at the perpetrators. The ring of adults would disperse, the grim faces approach, the hand reach down and grab the biceps too hard, and we would be hustled off to cars. And during all of this hullabaloo, the wronged girl would catch the glance of each of us, and there would be a triumphant smirk on her face.

And later would be the beating, mitigated by what our parents thought of the girl. When I was very small, I escaped punishment because Mother thought I was "too darned little" to know what was going on. This soon ceased to work. And these beatings were convincing. We only got up the courage to sneak into the weeds maybe once a year. Again it was all for the sake of science. We wanted to see if anything had changed. Pubic hair was regarded with great admiration.

"She'll tell," I warned my brother.

"Yeah, I know."

hired hands

To learn that the human condition is various, one only had to know the endless stream of men who came to work on our farm. Even then, America had a mainstream, the cities, where people got ahead, and a backwater, our farm, where people just drifted. The people who worked for us lived in tiny trailers behind our big red-roofed house or in tents. They slept in our home, in the room which would become mine eventually, and which smelled of smoke for years afterwards. They lived in the dank rooms in the basement, where the monstrous heater breathed.

Red's wife lost her legs in a heater explosion. Dennis Argotsinger, from Indiana, brought women from town into one of the trailers and bragged afterwards about what he had done to them. "She said no, but I just pushed her back, then she said yes, yes, yes." We were bug-eyed.

Rusty couldn't read but had the prettiest wife, beautiful black-haired Goldie. Both were from Arkansas, refugees from chicken-plucking plants. Dale Rice, just out of the Army, where he had been stationed in Korea, filled our heads with stories of "snapping pussy" — a variety known, he said, only in the

Orient. Some appeared so briefly that they seem in my memory
to have been spontaneously generated from cigarette smoke,
whiskey fumes, and patched blue jeans. Others were my Uncle
Johnny; and Long John; Leonard Bashford, a sheep shearer from
Fort Collins, who would drive nothing but black Dodges; another, a nameless dirty old man who rolled Prince Albert while
Work-a-Day juice dribbled through his chin stubble; Willard
Schenck, who practiced a secret vice; Bay Window, who read
muscle magazines and had groping hands; the Dirkies, whose
beautiful daughter we spied on through a slit in the sheetrock
around the downstairs shower and who didn't mind; Mexican
beet crews and their smoldering Mexican daughters; Garcia and
the three wetback brothers, who never said anything but "neep,
neep, neep"; Henry (Hank) Hess, who claimed to be a former
Hollywood film editor and who took me at sixteen to the
whorehouses in Lamar, Colorado where my virginity was lost;
and Lanky and his wife, Alice, the dirtiest woman who ever
lived, according to my father and my Uncle Raymond. These
were the stars, the most memorable, but on and on they march,
workers for a month, a week, or only a few days.

And these drunken, smoking drifters influenced me beyond
measure. Some had seen the world, and they brought with them
bawdy songs, stories of faraway places, and a willingness to in-
struct my brother and me in the genteel art of sex.

As I said, many of them simply materialized on the farm.
Some were, as my father said, "dragged out of the employment
office," a storehouse of human flotsam, as far as he was concerned. His problem in recruiting men was that he was incapable
of discretion. If a warm body showed up when he needed help,
he simply hired the body, though anyone could see he was hiring
trouble.

Not so long ago I sat in the kitchen as my father and mother
interviewed another new man and his wife. I had seen this scene
played out many times before. They came and went, sitting

nervously in our living room, on the edges of their chairs, hats on their knees.

Outside, about six hound dogs barked in the ancient Volvo in which they had arrived. Plainly, this man was no damned good. Hard knocks are etched in certain faces. He had that crafty, running away look of a dog who's done bad and won't come. The wife was nondescript. Nothing particularly wrong with her clothes or her appearance, but nothing particularly right either. She was simply a vessel into which a personality had never been poured, empty, like a cake pan stored on a shelf.

"How's your welding?" my father wanted to know.

The guy guessed he warn't no expert, but he warn't no slouch either.

He slid out his main chip, though he didn't need to; he was already hired and didn't know it.

"I welded quite a bit down at John Deere."

He waited for my father to digest this.

"Pretty good at welding, huh?"

The man nodded, and grinned.

"We work long hours, sometimes," said my father. "Any objection to that? Sometimes we'll work Sundays."

The guy said he didn't mind, as he nervously shifted his eyes to his wife.

She gave him a little nod. Probably, if they didn't get a paycheck soon, the dogs would starve.

She told my father she raised dogs. He wouldn't mind that, would he?

"You ain't gonna have them in the house, are you?"

"Oh, no. They'll be penned up."

Everything was decided quickly with handshakes all around and the wages set. They were to live in the old house on the farm. It is the domicile he selects for second-raters.

"What did you think, Bruce?" he asked after they left.

I thought it wasn't any of my affair. "Oh, no balls of fire, but they'll do all right," I said.

"I called his references," said Harold. "I think he laid it on a little thick about being at John Deere. He washed tractors and changed oil. Pete told me the only reservation he would have is the man has sticky fingers. I guess he had a drinking problem, too, but he's supposed to be over that."

"I'm sure he'll work out."

Later, after I told my wife about it, we roared with laughter.

"Here comes this guy in old turned up cowboy boots and faded blue jeans in an ancient Volvo full of hound dogs, and the only thing his references say is wrong with him is that he is a drunken thief, and my father hires him anyway. What a judge of character."

"Don't forget," my wife says.

"What?"

"You worked there, too."

My father would hire anyone. Everyone deserved a chance to show what he could do, even if all evidence indicated that it was nothing, because before the Big Farmers threw up their brick mansions in town and began living like lords behind acres of green lawn, farming had a certain egalitarianism.

Egalitarianism was natural to Harold because he was a landowner. Isn't a landowner equal to anyone? No banker or lawyer or even movie star or politician was above him. Harold was lord of his domain but usually too busy with practical tasks to make social distinctions. So even Dirty Ol' Bob was treated as an equal.

If you counted the encrustations on his overalls, Dirty Ol' Bob weighed 240 pounds. He had a drooping belly and a round red alcoholic's face shining with sweat and was deathly afraid of rattlesnakes. When Clark and I worked with him, staying upwind as much as possible, we carried rattlesnake rattles in our pockets, which we used with great success.

"You need more staples, Bob?" I'd ask, while Clark sneaked up behind him to shake the rattler. Bob would jump at the sound. By now Clark would have the rattles back in his pocket, and feigning fright myself, the two of us would poke around in the weeds looking for the "snake" while Dirty Ol' Bob perched atop a two-inch iron post with his black lace-up boots on the top barbed-wire. He'd crawl down gingerly, for he was deathly afraid of snakes and there might really be one in the weeds which grew along the fenceline. Such shenanigans carried on endlessly by us damaged Dirty Ol' Bob's pride.

He was probably about forty-four, and given to bragging about traveling to Denver's Larimer Street and waking with a whore so dirty the only pink spot was on her left tit, which he had been sucking. Bob would go to town for a minor drunk every month or so. Afterwards, when he was sleeping it off in the trailer, Father would haul us in there to see what a drunk looked like. Bob usually slept with our dog Rex licking his face. The dog found whatever oozed from it to be good. But all these minor drunks were just a prelude to his semiannual sojourn on Denver's Larimer St. during which he'd spend five months' pay.

But when tricked he acted just like a child.

"I'm going to tell your dad on you," he threatened after we had employed the rattles. He had guessed no real snake had been in the fence row by the smirks on our faces. For the next hour or so he refused to work with us, staying ahead of us on the fence line and looking back at us with sad, self-righteous resignation, like a tired cow.

In an hour or so, the inevitable happened. Harold came over the hill in whatever pickup he was driving that year, and Bob approached him for a man-to-man talk.

We could imagine what Bob was saying to him — that a man shouldn't be treated like that — and we were watching with a mixture of glee, dread, and curiosity, because no one could say what Harold would do.

As I said, a certain egalitarianism existed, but children should know their places. We had no business baiting a grown man and we knew it. Harold was clearly the boss, but man-to-man, the sorry alcoholic sack that was Bob and the then young, burly-chested, big-bellied landowner shared the equality of adults. But the complexity of it all was that we were the young lords of the farm, and we were being raised to be bosses too, as long as we didn't contradict Harold, and a boss-to-be could be forgiven for exercising his seignorial rights as a landowner, and scaring Dirty Ol' Bob up a fence post.

Besides, it was a story Harold could tell at the Elk's Lodge, for he would have one drink in those days and talk a little. Even younger, he had been known to come home from the Elk's Lodge slightly stinking himself, with tales about Father Zimkoski's latest shipment of Denver dancing girls, or of hitting the jackpot in the slot machine. Fun-loving Harold — the concept is a hard one for me to grasp. Still, thereafter, he kept his eye on us and told us in Bob's hearing we shouldn't treat a man like that. "You ain't no better than he is," he would say. This seemed to satisfy Bob.

And then one day, when we uncovered a real den of snakes, my father placed himself between Bob (now balanced again precariously atop a fence post) and the snakes and chopped off their heads with a flat-bladed shovel with as much emotion as a butcher whacking on hindquarters.

We hovered nearby for this bonanza of rattlers.

"You guys are just going to scare Bob with them. You can't have them."

Then why was he carefully removing the rattlers with his pocketknife?

"I'm putting these in the ashtray. You guys stay out of 'em."

But something in the way he said it made us aware that he really didn't expect us to. My father knew all about the irresistibility of rattles. He knew exactly where those rattlers would end up.

Dirty Ol' Bob took all his meals with us. At supper, usually long after dark, with the cows milked and a full day of fence fixing behind us and the dust wiped off our faces, we'd sit down to eat. My mother usually fixed fried chicken or fried steak or pot roast. Mashed potatoes were mandatory. Chicken was such a treat, eating it was almost stressful. Competition over the good pieces was fierce and the "men" got first choice. Mother tried to preside over this somewhat in the interest of fairness, but my father's attitude was that runts of the litter get hind tit. He believed in competition and Charles Darwin, except when it came to my sister, who always sat on Harold's left and got the wishbone. (While we were being trained in the roughshod world of men, Harold and Mother were engaged in convincing my sister she was a queen.)

So after the whining between my brother and me and the under-table kicks and blows subsided, and we had ingested enough mashed potatoes and chicken and canned string beans so that we knew at least today we would not die of starvation, the family banter began. Harold always sat at the head, my mother to the right, closest to the kitchen. My brother and I occupied the end and between us and the food was usually a ravenous crew of hired hands. It was a big table.

Harold might use it as a sort of bitching post, if he were in a bad mood. It was also the operations room, as Harold planned who would go where and who would do what in the morning, although usually the next day, after sniffing the morning air, he would completely change his mind. But sometimes he'd be in a playful mood.

"I checked that ashtray, and those rattlers weren't anywhere."

My brother kicked me on the ankle. Even in those days he was very serious about not being caught doing anything bad. He was so righteous and hardworking and good, so upright and crewcut and clean, and I so squirmy and ornery and just plain no damned good, everyone automatically assumed that whatever it was, I had done it.

"Maybe they rattled out," I giggled.

But Dirty Ol' Bob knew. He looked at us like he was atop a fence post. He knew where those rattlers were. Deep in our sweaty pockets, the bloody tips still oozing, or worse, in a paper sack so they'd rattle better. Probably we'd sneak down to his room tonight and shake that sack by his door. He hadn't had a proper drunk in a month, and all he dreamed about anyway was snakes.

sheep

Kansas State University, one of the three colleges my father attended, has been teaching for years that the most profitable farms are diversified. This was one of the lessons my father carried away with him from his years in agricultural schools. The same lesson has been passed on folklorically for generations. It's called "not having all your eggs in one basket." But it's a lesson slowly learned by many farmers.

Some catch on at the bank when the banker says, "I'm afraid if you're going to make a profit, you've got to start running stock."

Some never catch on and go broke.

Yes. Pure-dee big wheat farmers do make it, but the land's paid off. They have to watch their equipment expenses and not drive too new a pickup. But it is inevitable. Sooner or later a market calamity or hail or drought will severely crimp their styles.

"Diversified" means crops and livestock. I can imagine Harold mulling the matter over, see him squinting his eyes and squirming before he bought those first sheep. He had observed cattlemen spitting and fencing and riding and roping and sitting in the stock barn under a low ceiling of hats, and observed over time that only the best survived.

He had also made the astute observation that those who did survive, worked. And besides, didn't he carry away with him from Kansas State University a well-thumbed copy of *Sheep and Wool Science,* the 1933 edition? What could be a more thrifty animal for the farm? A sheep produced both wool and meat and made meat at least twice as efficiently as a steer. Probably, in his mind, he was already building mountainous mounds of wool and money in the bank. Hadn't the book claimed that, year for year, the well-managed herd of ewes made more than a herd of cows?

But he must have reached a conclusion of his own. The big cowmen worked. Work equals money. The more work, the more money. Sheep were more work than anything. "I'll be a sheepman."

I only remember that feeding bottle lambs was one of my earliest chores. And we kept up to three cows in the barn, milked by my brother and myself, to supply them. Ewes with twins didn't have enough milk for both and one was rejected, or the ewe died and we had to raise the orphaned lamb. What killed the ewe was infection — postpartum fever, or sometimes the womb would prolapse. These Harold shoved back in with his ungloved hand, and secured with hog rings. Survival was rare. Lambing went on and the dead ewes piled up in the corral. It took me not very long to discover that sheep were almost as interesting dead as alive.

When we were old enough, Clark and I were put to work in the barns. Anyone could stand in a corral gate, so there I stood, petrified with fright, the sheep running over me, through the gate and getting away. I got bigger though, and learned to stand in the gateway and whoop and wave my arms in a calisthenic jumping jack.

Clark, always bigger and able to do more, and with a better attitude, trudged along resignedly, his will being compressed more and more tightly within him by Father's. His very strength and size were his disadvantage. He was put to work younger than I. And all of this produced within him a martyr complex which plagued him until he died.

Lambing is brutal, trudging work. Somehow the operation had grown to over a thousand producing ewes. The big sheep barn, more than four thousand square feet, wasn't big enough then. A hundred ewes a day might give birth at the height of lambing. Each had to be penned in an individual stall for a day or so. That helped the ewe take the lamb, and we could check each animal for illnesses. In these small pens we could also trick ewes whose lambs were stillborn or died a few days after birth. We skinned out the dead lamb and tied the skin to an orphan lamb. It usually worked.

To keep track of this birthing bonanza, we used buckets of varicolored paints. The paint specially made for the job was designed not to wear off on a ewe, and so wouldn't wear off on us either. Each lamb had to be numbered, with a special symbol for twins, a double zero, and corresponding numbers for the ewes. When we got to a hundred, we changed colors. If we were clever, we got the ewe in the pen before she had her lamb. We'd cull through the crowd, calling out "that one." Once a ewe about to give birth was identified, we caught her by the hind leg with a hook on a long pole. It was easy to tell when a sheep was about to give birth — a cantaloupe-sized bag of yellow fluid would droop from the ewe's rear and then splosh on the ground. Then a little head would pop out.

This meant we spent all day dragging slimy ewes into pens along with their slimy wet progeny. We numbered, stumbled in straw and shit up to our knees when the corrals were wet, and removed tails and balls with a rubber band machine. I learned how to pinch upward, over the scrotum, and push the balls down, while the soft, floppy-eared lamb panicked with pain. I spread the band with the machine, feeling to make sure the balls were at the bottom of the scrotum, before I released the trigger. We used the banding device for tails, too. It cut off the circulation, so the tail would wither, and, after several weeks, drop off. The corrals were littered with mummified tails and scrotums. Ten seconds after we put the rubbers on, the lamb would be wagging its doomed tail as if nothing had happened. Sheep have such short memories.

We smelled like sheep. We probably smelled like sheep at school. The Seamans said there was nothing wrong with sheep, except they smelled so bad. Harold said the Seamans never liked the smell of money.

Our hired hands helped us with this work, most of them hating the sheep as much as we did. The sheep were a cause of high turnover. Among stockmen, cattlemen were the aristocracy, hog growers were next in status, and sheepmen came last. The hands felt doubly damned. Not only was the work hard, they couldn't even talk about it when they went into town. Some actually beat the sheep. Harold shook his head at the letting go of so many good workers. "They just can't work with sheep," he said.

But Walter Tate could. He was tall and thin and stooped and hawk-beaked and wild-haired and red-faced and he didn't drink or smoke or cuss and he loved his mother. He had big knobby wrists and huge hands which dangled from the sleeves of a plaid flannel shirt. He wore the same coveralls as Harold, the brown ones which make farmers hard to distinguish from mud.

On the surface Walter seemed simple-minded, and he probably was. When Julene was small, she was constantly in his trailer, fondling the lambs, and later, as she grew, he helped her with her horses. With both animals and children, Walter had the touch. He joked that he was going to wait until Julene grew up, and then marry her and perhaps that was in his simple dreams. As she began to sprout breasts, at a time when she was already moving into her own world of horse clubs, barrel racing and school chums, Harold began to worry. He thought the relationship had gone too far, and ordered Julene to stay away from him. This was something my sister told me later that Walter never understood.

For years he herded our sheep, living in a tiny wheeled cabin in the big pasture, penning the sheep at night and watching over them during the day. He lived with our dogs, training them. The first to receive his tutelage was Rex, who had grown up without the benefit of Walter's teaching and was more interested in his pecker than anything else. He'd prowl neighboring farms for days, coming back sore-footed and exhausted. But Walter made a sheep dog of Rex. He'd stand in the corral gate with me and the two of us could sometimes stop a herd of stampeding wethers.

Seeing Walter work with Rex gave Harold the Great Idea. He sent away for a hundred-dollar Australian sheep dog and gave the dog to Walter to raise. And Walter trained the animal until it could go around the herd either way, work in a pen, stand in a gate, and do so with such constant eagerness, that whenever she could, Lady herded sheep by herself. As Walter without qualm took baby lambs to warm in his hut.

It is the way we all begin to understand the various paths of life. I had scorned and scoffed at his ways and teased him because he was simple. But planted in my mind now, sneakily invading years later from nowhere, there is Walter, the root of my definition of gentleness.

our place — the other place

It must have been about 1965. I was home from college in
disgrace. On the way home from a North River bar in Lawrence,
I upset a "Stop for Pedestrians in the Crosswalk" sign. Being a
good citizen, I parked to set it upright again. A cop watched the
whole while. He gave me an offer I should have accepted.

"I'll let you go if you walk home."

"But it's raining."

He got that what-can-you-do-with-them look, and I was
handcuffed. In the police station, I tried to work out my blood
alcohol content with calculus in my attempt to determine if I
should assent to taking the test they wanted to give me, but the
figures wouldn't come out right. I woke up in jail. Somewhere in
that nightmare, a university dean of men poked his head inside. It
was standard procedure for him to do that, I realize now. If you
turned out to be the son of someone who could contribute to
the school — and the dean could tell those by simply opening
his patrician nostrils and sniffing the sodden wretch within the
cell — the matter was handled quietly with some "ha-has" and
some "boys will be boys." But if you were poor pickings, the university threw you to the wolves. I was in jail during finals. It was a
bad semester. No driver's license, and I was kicked out of school.

I was home in disgrace but it was no longer my home. We had moved. We were temporarily living in my Uncle Wilbur's house. My grandfather, Ferdinand Fernando, had died several years before, and the estate he had left behind was crumbling. His son Raymond sold his inheritance as quickly as he could. He and his wife Cookie were spending the money on red convertibles. My Uncle Johnny, Harold's youngest brother, tried farming but his efforts ran downhill like a gully in clay. My beautiful Aunt Berneice, a widow, held on to hers, but Harold farmed much of it. Aunt Alta, the oldest of the children, lived in Alaska, but after inheriting her share, she sold her Kansas land and bought a farm in Missouri. And Wilbur, Harold's older brother, was in trouble with the bank.

For years Wilbur had farmed next to "The Other Place," on one of the finest sections in the state. This had been more or less given to him by Fernando. No one ever remembered him making a payment. After Grandfather died, Wilbur got clear title to his land, and on such land, banks are eager to lend.

Wilbur was a wonderful humorist, guitar player, and man, but he wasn't much of a farmer. His best jokes live on in our family legends. He said he was the first strip farmer in our county. "I plant it and the grasshoppers strip it." It was said of him that if the hitch broke, leaving the machine he was towing behind, Wilbur wouldn't notice it until he ran over it on the next round. Sometimes he didn't notice it then.

"Our Place" was an amalgam of rented and owned land divided out of John Oliver's estate. Mother owned some of it. Her sister Helen owned a half-section, and her brother Leonard owned a quarter. The rest, about a section, was owned by Grandma Carlson.

We farmed mostly wheat. Harold got two-thirds, and the owners got a third. When Grandma Carlson died, the land had to be divided, and the division precipitated such a fight with

Jasmin's sister Irene, who lived bordering us, that the two didn't speak for thirty years.

My brother and I, Harold, and Henry Hess — a man with a magnificent handlebar moustache, the man who had personally driven me to a Colorado whorehouse where in ten seconds I had lost my virginity ("so long, Bub," said the whore) — and maybe Dirty Ol' Bob built the fence between the two properties. The land had been surveyed for the division, and the markers were clearly visible.

"I'd like to build it right on the line," my father fumed. But he built it a foot on our side. We learned a lot about fencing that day. How to drive double steeples to act as fence guides so we could stretch wire through gullies. And it was just as well Harold took the precaution of building a foot short because we'd never had to sight a fenceline through such precipitous terrain before, and the fence turned out crooked.

Our Place had old problems. It wasn't the best land, and it was hilly. We couldn't travel directly to our other place because the intervening creek had washed out the road. This added miles each year as we moved machinery. And the soil on some of the land was poor. One of the fields bordered the creek that had taken out the road. The old bridge pilings are still rotting in the draw. It was about a half-section, but who could tell? It was squeezed against an equally deep ditch on the east, and fenced off to keep the cows out of wherever someone thought it was flat enough to farm.

I do remember a scary corner of that field. It was a diagonal, not a square turn, into a gully. You went into it going down and came out of it going up, so the tractor had to be shifted into a lower gear or it would die. We built up our belly muscles pulling the clutch. Atop the field was a sandy spot where years ago Grandma Carlson had transplanted iris. The small blue and yellow varieties had survived and would bloom each spring. When I was younger, Mother would sometimes drive us out to see them, her hand on her hat to keep it from blowing away, and her print dress blowing between her legs.

I suppose that and the pasture and the land on the other side against the good gravel road must have added up to a section. We farmed another section on the other side of the road, mostly good flat land with only one serious gully running through it. Two more quarters lay to the south of our house. One was all grass, with a magnificent forty-acre buffalo wallow at its bottom. Early on, Harold simply left it alone, but since it looked as rich as the Mississippi Delta, he finally broke it out. It was hourglass shaped. Harold said the only problem with it was "you either get a crop or you don't." A buffalo wallow is always likely to have moisture, but every other year runoff will fill them with rainwater — this one to about four feet in depth. Then we would get out the motorboat and ski. When it was full of water we called it Lake Lizzie.

A hilly quarter bordered the "lagoon quarter." It was what you would call "feed ground." The soil was too poor to grow wheat. And across the gravel road, to the south of the "good section," was a quarter marred only on one side by erosion and a second quarter of good flat land.

The land, the two-story red-roofed home, the flower-filled yard, the big elm trees out back, the north windbreak planted by us, the windmill tower with the hawk's nest, the dusty shop, the big red barn, the rickety outbuildings — that was "Our Place."

But we were always being carried in the pickup to "The Other Place," or driving tractors between both. Between The Other Place and Our Place was the "Badcock Quarter" with its deteriorating house on one corner, once lived in by Babcocks. Whenever we said "Badcock" quarter, Mother would wrinkle her nose.

The Other Place, which became "The Farm," bordered my Uncle Wilbur's. Wilbur's place sat on a fine, flat section of land. We owned the land across the road from him both ways. Wilbur was going broke and he and Harold made a deal. Harold would trade Our Place for his place and bail him out of debt. We would move to town and drive to the new place, a distance of twenty miles.

I don't know how the argument went, or even if there was one. I only know that for years Mother had sat at the living room table drawing plans of houses. She liked ours, but the dirt got in. And it was cold and consumed at times a thousand gallons of propane a month, cascading into the breathing monster downstairs. (At least it was better than the coal we used to have.) So in the middle of the biggest move of our lives, my parents were building Mother's dream house in Goodland. In the meantime, we had to move out, into Wilbur's old house. It was as magnificently dark, roomy and spacious as ours, with rooms upstairs off a staircase, but you had to go through the kitchen to go to the bathroom. At twenty, I certainly didn't want to live there. I had become a prisoner there of my parents, the most humiliating fix a twenty-year-old boy can be in.

Eventually, I returned to college, and in the summer, as usual, came home for another healthy injection of John Deere driving. My parents had moved into their new home. Our Place was now Wilbur's, and The Other Place had now truly become "The Farm."

I had made a collegiate comeback at one of my father's old schools, Kansas State University, and never had trouble with grades again. My first summer on "The Farm" was also the summer of James Harold Shaver, Mary McMasters, and Suze.

I don't know how it happened. Shaver was mixed up in it. All I know is that I got into the back seat of a car with Susan, and it was all over in thirty seconds. I was in love without reservation. Suddenly, all my worries were canceled, and I was having fun. I probably worked for my father that summer almost willingly. I don't even remember working. Somehow, Susan and I were together most of the time. By the end of the summer we were engaged. What a summer! The aftertaste of it lingered on through two more semesters and a marriage, which went downhill fast.

Shaver was a moggy fellow in those days, almost like a Labrador pup. Most of the time Susan and I would find him with Mary and her pint of Southern Comfort. I had my car back by then. We'd get beer and go to the lake. Shaver wouldn't swim. He was so disgusted by the practice he would skim flat stones at

Mary, making her get out of the water. Then he would neck with her on the roof of the car. Susan and I were more circumspect. We usually waited until after dark, and during the day we played in the water. She loved it.

She had a big, wide mouth with a scar over her lip which made her look worldly and sexy. She wore her hair long, and it had body, so at times she looked like a model. But when she popped out of the water with her hair stringing down, her big wide face made her look like a chipmunk or a beaver. This made me laugh. She had a mind, and later proved herself in business. She had it and she knew it and she showed it, in a blue bikini. Anyone would have fallen.

My Uncle Johnny told Harold that bikinis were made for looking, "So I looked," he said.

"God," said Harold in reference to the event. I had landed a whopper.

Whoever was looking, Susan didn't seem to mind. To dances she wore short shorts and knotted-down kerchief tops. Burly-chested boys with leather vests would try to steal her from me. They'd give me the one-eyed bull look while chatting with Susan. But she was always faithful, though her habit of taking a single, lingering, thoughtful look backwards was sometimes disturbing to me.

We drove home from one of those dances in the rain one night but didn't make it. We parked behind the Edson school while the thunderstorms boomed and were soon naked in the backseat.

"What the hell," she said. The rain came down in buckets. She got out and we danced, her wet hair making her look like that chipmunk or that beaver. What chance did I have after that? This remains the most exhilarating night of my life.

And that should have been the end of it. That great summer. We slogged through two more semesters of college together.

Somehow, I convinced her to transfer from K.U. to K. State. I was working as a graduate assistant to Dr. Elmer Hiney then, but we weren't getting along.

I worked with a crew of high school kids as Hiney's technical assistant. Hiney wasn't around that much, which made the job tolerable. We'd cut the tiny plots of wheat the old way, with sickles, binding it by hand with twine. The purpose was to gather seed from each carefully bred variety. Sometimes we'd follow behind a tiny swather, tying the bundles as they dropped and placing a paper sack over the heads to keep the seed pure. It was all fed into a tiny threshing machine. When the threshing was done, the seed was put in a white bag with a label tied to the top and stored in endless rows of shelves in dank basements where I believe most of it eventually rotted. It was government work.

It was hard work, but I had been trained to love work. Mosquitoes everywhere, with afternoon temperatures over a hundred. We were in the fields at dawn, and did not leave until sundown. I did this work well, managing my crew of high school students by example. I could out-tie them, I could out-scythe them. Even Hiney saw that I was a worker.

In my mind, I compared Hiney to my father. They both drove men hard in harvest, but Hiney didn't throw wrenches, or cuss. Instead he nailed me with withering comments on my character in front of the high school boys I was supposed to manage. I knew what he thought of me and he was right about one thing — I was not cut out for wheat breeding.

Susan and I were happy for a while. Her sense of humor was as good as mine, and we laughed our way through our troubles. But it was early evident we were headed for divorce. Her childhood had been poor and insecure. I had never worried about provision. She was driven to make it, worried constantly about her weight, and swallowed Benzedrine for it while I drank my beer. I wanted to slow down; she wanted to speed up. She presented me with a budget book, which I tried to keep but couldn't. We argued over every dime. She wanted new furniture and a China hutch. What for, I would say, we'll just have to pack it? We both knew in six months it wasn't going to last. The humor became bitter and our jokes were on each other.

I decided to give up my graduate assistantship. I wasn't going to live the next three years under another despot like my father. We decided to blow Manhattan and go to K.U. But we had no money. We commuted at first from an apartment built into an old school building nine miles out, in a Volkswagen. I worked in the library and put numbers on stadium seats. Vietnam loomed over everything. I don't know how it happened but I had no deferment. Graduate school was pointless.

To the most important question of my generation, Vietnam, I responded mostly with whining, as did many others. One day I would whine that I was going to Canada. The next day I would declare I had no deferment because I didn't believe student deferments were fair to poor blacks in ghettos. The strain was so great I began talking, when drunk, in an English accent. Susan called this an affectation, but I couldn't stop doing it. We fought and fought, once daring one another to risk death by crawling along a narrow rotten ledge on a rickety building.

By now we had moved to a tiny house a few blocks from campus. I applied for jobs, but couldn't get them. I was 1-A. The draft board kept grabbing me. I'd had a couple of physicals, but both times I'd been saved on technicalities.

But time was running out. A reserve unit was called up, and I took the place of the lab technician who worked at National Alfalfa. I kept books and ran tests to determine how much protein and vitamin A were in samples of alfalfa pellets. And the pay was almost decent.

At last the bastards got me, in June 1968. The night before I reported, Susan and I made love. I think it was for old times' sake. In the morning, she cried.

"I just have this feeling I'll never see you again."

And I was thinking, "Thank God."

Of course I missed her so bad that in three days I called her and whined and wanted her to come and be with me, but she wouldn't. Beware of summer love.

She got most of my pay for a year and a half, but when I made sergeant, I could say where my money went. I stopped contributing the 60 percent of my pay that had gone to her. I had been dead broke for eighteen months. That stirred her up one more time. I was called into the Provost Marshall's office.

"I hear you're not sending any money to your wife," he said.

"The bitch won't live with me," I replied. He shrugged. Who cares? And that was the end of that, and all use of myself to her.

The divorce papers didn't catch up with me until after I was out of the army. The sheriff caught me on a dusty road. I was back home. I was having a hiatus.

I'd worked for a time in Alaska, with the state Department of Fish and Game. My job there was catching crabs, measuring the shells and weighing the guts. This was called biology. The boss was a ramrod Mormon, who wanted my ruler placed on the same spot on the desk every morning. I'd been through the army. I'd been through a marriage. I'd been through the mill, and by now I knew the world shelled out an inordinate number of asses. And I was a bit older and some things just weren't worth it.

I hitchhiked the Alcan Highway. In Seattle, I spent my last hundred dollars on a '52 Chevy. I paid for gas with an old Gulf credit card, and I hadn't eaten in two days when I got home. No one seemed too glad to see me.

The army owed me unemployment. I was in the doorway of the state office when a friend drove by and asked if I wanted to go to Denver. I hopped inside. The guy was wanted on drug charges in Kansas and was clearing out. This is how I became a member of the Hays, Kansas refugees of 1971 — all students on the lam. Here I found serious acid. I leapt into it like a swimmer.

The thrill of acid is self-limiting, though. Usually those who take it wake up one morning and say, "Jesus, I don't want any more of *this* shit," and they quit. It happened in our group, which graduated quickly to amphetamines and cocaine and came perilously close to heroin. I stuck mostly with pot and deteriorated more slowly. Then I got back into beer.

That I was actually accepted into this crowd for a brief period is proof of degeneracy. Still, I retained weapons. My tongue was sharp. My wit was keen. I'd have them laughing on the floor in their flannel shirts and hair and big heavy boots amid the crab-infested army surplus sleeping bags. I could get them.

And then I would tell them the truth. "That joke I just told wasn't any good, Tater," I'd say. "If you get any more pickled, you won't have a brain at all."

Which would usually cause hysteria.

But I wasn't really a hippie, ever. Just a pretender. I wasn't cool. I was kicked out because no one who wouldn't deal cocaine could be trusted. And then I was gone, saved by what I had learned on the farm. I caught a job with a wheat-cutting crew.

We were a broken-down outfit filled with broken-down people, and we cut wheat. We cut it from Texas to Montana and we had fun and made money. The wheat finally cured me of Susan. But of course I came back home broke, in an old Nash Rambler.

Rambler is what I had become. I had no money, so mostly I rambled around in my head. And of course I was horny. I don't know how long I stayed around Goodland. I worked in the beet factory in the winter and put up steel buildings in the summer.

In the winter, out of work most of the time, I bundled together with my fellows in a tiny pink house, slept all day and, at night, sought sex. Our only goal was to score. Score sex, score dope, score money, even if we worked for it seventy hours a week at the beet factory. Here is where I learned of the underbelly of every small town. Wages are low, waitresses are married to tire busters and live in tiny houses with squalling children and hound dogs. The desperation threw us all out on the streets, where we congregated on empty corner lots to save gas. What was going on was dope deals, what was going on was hastily made trips with young girls in old cars, what was going on was the surreptitious passage of the wine bottle. The cops eyed us. We waved back nonchalantly.

But what cannot be described is the darkness of it, lost in time where life goes nowhere. I wrote a story at the time that, while fiction, may be true enough. An excerpt:

She was the wife of a railroader and the victim of complete genetic baldness. Her wig was askew. Darnel eased the coupe into low and pulled behind her. She was coy with us as we pursued her, tossing her acrylic locks and accelerating with loud squeals when the light changed.

"She's frisky tonight," said Darnel.

We pursued her down the near-deserted street and caught her at the light. Once she was caught, the results were always the same.

"Come on boys, get off my tail. What if my husband hears you been chasing me?"

"Ain't he on the road?" said Darnel.

"What if somebody sees us?"

"No one will see us at your place."

"OK, but no hanky-panky."

We followed her home where she took off her clothes and her wig. She had us on the living room couch because the kid was asleep in the one bedroom. Without a trace of hair on her body, she was as smooth as a bowling pin. Darnel looked at me when I finished, and lifted his eyebrows like an epicurean. He went back for seconds. I watched from the kitchen table and had a cup of coffee.

A vision burst upon me. I was no longer in a dreary cottage with the north wind rattling the windows, watching sex lit by a bulb dangling from a cord. I was roaring down the highway. I rushed through the sweet scent in the air at a tremendous speed. My torso was naked and I was tanned. I was hot and loose. I was riding a Harley into the sun and would never see Goodland again.

I needed a girl or I would grow crazy. The ones I found were caught in the same pointless life as mine, drifting on Main Street, looking to score. The beet factory got me out of there. I saved my pay and went back to K.U. in a '58 Buick hardtop that I paid three hundred bucks for. I had the G.I. bill and tuition and enrolled in journalism school.

I was poverty-stricken. My apartments were even meaner than those I had inhabited at K. State. I drove a taxi and had a thousand other jobs I can't remember. I would do anything. I got back on at National Alfalfa, this time on the end of scoop. I walked a lot because I couldn't afford gas. I was hard, and I met Kris.

Jimmy Shaver was also at K.U. We were in the Gaslight Tavern, my haunt from earlier days, but the acid bubble had broken and the atmosphere was no longer friendly. Still, I drank there sometimes. It was cheap. Jimmy Shaver's wife, Adele, introduced me and Kris. Jimmy and Adele were in the Gaslight one night with two of her college friends when I walked in.

"I need a girl," I said. "Who's going to go out with me?"

The one with red hair declined. But Kris said yes. And from then on, I could not really pry her loose from me.

I only made it through one semester. I got an "A" and an incomplete. Back in Goodland, I'd sold a lid of Kansas pot to an undercover agent for five dollars. I'd told him it wasn't any good, but he insisted. And I was out of beer.

Months later, the bust came down and I was taken back to

Goodland in chains. Harold bailed me out and Mother was bawling and preachers were coming to the house. Kris stood by me. I went back to Lawrence to await my fate and finished the semester. The law was kinder then and the charges were dropped.

I had been accepted into the Peace Corps. The lure of adventure was too strong. I went to Brazil. I was a dismal failure at it, and went into yellow-bellied cultural shock at about the sixth month. I drank too much, and consorted with whores, all the time keeping up a correspondence with Kris. I loved Brazil. I loved to look at it. I loved to write about it on foldup airmail envelopes. At the end I got so bad I was crying when I passed the shops of tiny coffins and watched the scrawny women dressed in rags pull the water-filled barrel from the well. "Five cents a liter," they would cry.

At the last I did what the priest's dog did. I followed the shade. I had it over the dog, though, since I carried a bottle of Brahma Chop. I thought of Dirty Ol' Bob and, drunk, played with the kids that came by all day. I got so sad I had to come home.

I was curiously undaunted by this utter failure. I brought back a bottle of Brazilian sugarcane alcohol and souvenirs for all. I bought Kris a necklace, from which dangled a purple stone carved into a tiny fist — a good luck charm in Brazil. And for others, I brought Brazilian hammocks. And then I regaled them for days with my tales.

I moved into a dismal hole and scooped more for National Alfalfa. At last, Kris let me make love to her. We weren't very good at it in the beginning but we got better. It was getting serious. At last, I made the call.

"Dad," I said. "You know I'm not getting anywhere. How about trying me out on the farm?"

"You'll have to work like anyone else," he said.

Kris said she would come and live with me when she got out of school in the spring. And she did. By that time, I was striding bigger than life over the land, and I was hard.

sugar beets

Kris and I lived together in a second-floor apartment. It was on the corner of the building and had views both ways and a breeze most of the time. We had a bedroom, kitchen, and living room, and unlike my places in Lawrence, the plumbing worked. Soon we knew everyone in the building and had them all connected to cable television, running 18-gauge wires from the back of our set to everyone else's.

Harold would come stomping in every morning before seven. He liked to haul his men to the farm. That way, none of us could escape. We were farming sugar beets. The beets had Big Farmers running everywhere, and the crisp March air smelled like fresh dollar bills.

Sugar beets are a curious crop. As far as I can figure, farmers get rich on them because America hates Cuba. Of course, if war broke out, we'd need a domestic supply. It's a strategic commodity, used for so many things.

The sugar beet brought jobs. Just out of the army, I had worked putting up the big plant, painting beams orange. The builders were in such a hurry, they hired anyone. Sometimes, when I asked what to do next, the boss became so exasperated he'd say, "Get lost." I'd sneak away for the day, coming back to punch out. Good work if you can get it.

The money flowed, the big steam shovels dug, the skeleton of the factory rose eighty feet from the plains, and two Mexican workers were sailed off the top of it on a windy day, still clinging to a big blue sheet of tin. Great Western Sugar was a'coming. Blue. With the white GW on the package so big it made you proud.

It was all some big subsidized deal, with the government stirring the paddle. Farmers had to apply for an allotment, and once they got it, keep asking for more, until sugar beets made them rich, or until they went broke raising them. Sugar beets are what is called an investment-intensive crop, meaning they cost a lot of money to grow. Since the beets grow below the ground, they were not susceptible to hail, the hazard which prevents the irrigated Plains from being the vegetable garden of the world.

The plant at its peak contracted for 55,000 acres of beets, beets hauled in by tandem-axle farm trucks and semis from as far as eighty miles away. My father grew three hundred of these acres. A good beet crop beats twenty tons an acre and might contain twenty percent sugar. If you got twenty dollars a ton for them you could feel good, but in 1972 or '73, when wheat reached five dollars a bushel, beets went to fifty-five dollars. Multiply, and take a good look at all those zeros. Farmers were running for the U.S. Senate and buying condominiums in Colorado, skiing with President Ford. And they thought it would never end.

Bob Hurt and I grew the beets. Bob was a big-bellied man out of Texas, but nothing about him was soft. He could pick up a weighted tractor tire and balance it on end, muscling it around to fit the axle. He was also what my father called a religious fanatic because he liked to go to church on Sunday. He had a big, plain face, the kind you wear to the Serious Branch of the Southern Baptist Church. God was mean as hell, and he'd get you if you didn't toe the mark. It was not easy to make Bob laugh. His idea of humor was a skunk coming out of my end of an irrigation pipe.

Kris cooked for me and stood by me in my conflicts with Harold. She was smart, and I could talk to her. She wasn't beautiful, but look what happened the last time. I was beginning to fall in love with her. We were talking marriage.

Bob was aghast at it all. To be working with a fornicator, and one who probably smoked pot besides, and, just like his father, was a heathen, even if he did call himself an agnostic. "They's rules, boy," he said, "and you're going to find out about them."

Still, working with a man who laughs once a month is better than working with one who doesn't laugh at all. Our other hand, Uncle Raymond, didn't laugh a bit. As we rode with Harold together to work each morning, Uncle Raymond would lean on me in a druidical stupor.

"Raymond, goddamn it," I'd say, and he'd get off me for a few seconds, and go right back into his stupor. After a few weeks, I gave up, resigned to it.

We had moved up in the farming world considerably by then, driving air-conditioned row crop John Deeres, 4320s and other combinations of big numbers, and our summer fallow tractor was a 6030 (the Sixty-thirty) which could handily pull a five-bottom plow and cut the time for disking a quarter to about one day.

Raymond drove the 6030 because, according to my father, he didn't like to think. Harold called him his tractor dog. Raymond didn't like row crops. The thought of driving over a stalk of corn or a blade of milo paralyzed him with fright.

Things never worked out for Uncle Raymond. My grandfather had heaped farms and ranches on him, even a slice of paradise in Arkansas, with a big ranch home and a fishing pond. But Raymond lost it all. My father put him to work, and he and his wife, Cookie, and their children lived in the old farm home for a few years, arguing behind the cracked asbestos shingles.

When Grandfather died, Raymond along with the rest of his children inherited a big chunk of money, and he left. He and Cookie drove red Chevy convertibles until the money was gone, and then she left him. An incident occurred after Raymond had been drinking in a bar on Goodland's south end, and he wound up in jail for a few months. After that, whatever pride he had had disappeared, and he shuffled back to our farm for refuge. Never did the concept of "work" weigh so heavily on a man, but he worked simply because he had no will. As in the old days with my brother and me, Dad kept an eye on him.

"Raymond's tahrd," he'd explain. And would give him time off.

Raymond was faithful. He'd drive the 6030 all summer. The job required little more thought than onewaying. We disked now, then undercut. We had begun to save straw cover. Our machines had grown wings, because now they were too wide for the road. The wings were lowered with levers, and it was now possible to farm over two hundred acres a day with the cultivators.

Raymond seldom got that much done. The machines were so wide that it was difficult to gauge a perfect lap, and Raymond never bothered and farmed half the field twice. Nor could he drive straight. I would take over for him at noon, wasting an hour to straighten things out.

Raymond was on Mellaril. The drug eliminated his emotional swings but made him into a zombie and allowed him to enjoy his favorite pastime, which was looking into his mouth in the rearview mirror. Raymond wasn't physically strong, and the Mellaril, or his general depressed condition, gave him a shuffling walk, like he'd spent years in irons. This made it almost impossible to work in unison with him. It was harder lifting pipe with him than lifting it alone. He got out of a lot of hard work because of this.

So this was our crew. Raymond, Bob Hurt, Dad, and myself, and below us on the plain lay the flat, gray fields which would become the 330 acres of sugar beets, 200 acres of corn, and 100 odd acres of pinto beans and milo. Bob looked at it with resignation. A good Christian wears his yoke. The sight of it caved Raymond in. I was, at thirty-three, still busy trying to please my father. I was the farmer apprentice, my lace-up boots striding bigger than life over the land. That is, when I wasn't over the hill in the pickup smoking a pipe of pot. And Harold rubbed his hands together with relish because there was work to do.

Kris and I made the decision and set the marriage date. I was going to be a Big Farmer some day. A sugar beet farmer.

werk

To grow sugar beets, the land must be deep-plowed. I did that job in the fall with the big 6030, working at it until the ground became so hard it would break the blades. This officially ended the farming season and it was time to put away the plow.

Such was my enthusiasm then that I would say things like "Better get to plowing." But trouble was brewing — the same kind that brews on any farm. My theory was that if I worked steadily at something the job would get done. Harold's theory was to work until it was done. I drove until six or seven in the evening and quit. This caused bitter arguments. When the others drove, somehow fewer acres were covered, and on most days they quit earlier than I did, always under the impression they hadn't. I pointed this out as evidence of the superiority of my system. I was told I was young and could take it.

Usually, we didn't get the plowing finished before the ground froze. We plowed again in the spring, though every acre finished in the fall was appreciated. Sugar beets went in as early as March 15, no later than mid-April.

So there we stood. Fifteen, maybe twenty operations from a million dollars. Raymond had his Mellaril, I had my pot, Bob had God, and Harold had his work. What a crew.

We were learning something new about soils. If tons of nitrogen and phosphorous fertilizers are put on them, and mixed, and watered and stirred, they tend to form aggregates. These aggregates are called clods. Artificial fertilizers either accelerate the degradation of organic material, or kill the living portion of it. One could surmise, like my father, that if the corn wasn't killed by the fertilizers and chemicals, the soil organisms, which were protected below the surface, likely wouldn't be either. But earthworms do come to the surface after fertilization and watering, and die. So something goes on below the soil surface that farmers don't know much about.

If conditions were perfect, the packer, which was towed over the ground after plowing, would break up the clods. It was a twelve-foot machine, equipped with two rows of heavy rollers, one behind the other. The center of each roller was surrounded with a ring of metal teeth. All of this was designed to mash the plowed ground flat again, returning it roughly to the condition it was in before we had plowed it. You plowed in the fall to loosen the soil and packed in the spring to tighten it up again. All manner of reasons were given for doing it this way. You plowed to break up the hard pan and turn the weed seeds under, but you packed to flatten the plow rows and make the soil firm enough so the water would run in rows. But in fact it was done that way because that was the way we had always done it. And because the Great Western Sugar Co., Inc. advised it. When the neighbor didn't get his plowing done, and his beets were better than ours, it didn't prompt Harold to rethink his practices. He had the best argument in the world: a paid off, four thousand-acre farm.

But conditions were seldom perfect. They were seldom even close. What we normally had after the packer passed once,

maybe twice, sometimes three times, was a flat expanse of wal-
nut-sized clods, four inches deep.

Packing so early in the spring was cold work. Packer work
was also mindless work, just right for Raymond. The soil was
packed one way, then the other. The only problem was telling
where you'd been. The soil was gradually reduced from dark,
earth-smelling plow rows to a dead gray expanse of dust-deviled
flatness. In a lucky year, a rain would come then, and loosen
everything up — "melting the clods," according to Harold. But
most of the time it didn't rain.

Harold is a digger. Most good farmers are. He digs and digs.
He straightens up from the digging and looks at the horizon.
He's got his jaw locked sideways, and a muscle is bulged out
below his cheek. He looks and looks. "He's gonna water, ain't he,
Bob?" I say.

Bob allows himself a little sigh. God knows men are weak-
fleshed.

"Better get your boots on, boy," he says. This is high good
humor to him, watching me squirm at the thought of the work
ahead.

"Onward Christian soldiers, marching off to war," I sing.

Harold has ceased dipping and digging and is driving down
the access row between the irrigated quarters. The dust streams
from behind. The wind is blowing. It's blown all spring.
Sometimes in it are little chunks of ice, which pepper my face.

Harold is coming up the hill. Bob and Raymond and I are
standing in the shop. Raymond fades into the back, to examine
his mouth in a rearview mirror. It's so dim back there he can't
possibly see anything.

"Better check your shovel, Boy," says Bob. In those days I was
five-six and 145 pounds. Bob goes six feet and some and 240. But
I'm wiry and will try to work all summer as hard as he does, even
if I'm doomed to crack. But it is still early in the spring and my

enthusiasm hasn't yet been rubbed out by weariness. The muscles across my chest are taut and my belly is springy.

"It's ready," I say, in my ready-for-anything western voice. It's the same kind of voice used to say, "I'll just climb up on that elevator and cut that six-inch bar off with a torch." Big Farmers can do anything.

Bob had already taught me about shoveling. "The trouble with you, boy, is nobody has ever taken the time to learn you."

He was right. We spent hours. He taught me. I think he got enjoyment out of it.

I'm a quick learner. The lessons begin as he says, "Well, you take this here," and I watch. The next time I can do it myself.

What I 'take here' most often is my irrigation shovel. I review in my mind his lessons. An irrigation shovel should be almost flat. It is not a garden spade. It shouldn't have a foot ridge on the blade, at the top. That catches mud. The tip should be filed almost straight, so it's about three inches wide, and sharp. It should be polished until it shines. When I go in hardware stores, I eye shovels. The five-dollar discount model just won't do. If I could find one, I'd try one of those forty-dollar aluminum spades, though Bob says the stainless steel kind is best. Harold thinks this is all silly. A shovel is a shovel. But he's wrong.

Bob has taught me how to push and turn the mud, and turn over the shovel, so the load slides. His mud rows look almost troweled, and mine are beginning to.

"You push it. You don't lift it." Which is what an irrigation shovel is made for. "Shoving moves more mud than lifting" should be the anthem of irrigation.

But I've added another. "You have to think like water."

I look out the shop door and wonder if there's enough time to slip behind the upright silo and smoke another bowl of pot, but Harold is driving into the yard.

He thinks we better melt down those clods ourselves.

Raymond is shuffling up, smoking a Kool. He smokes five packs a day.

"I don't think it's gonna rain. If we don't soak up that ground, we'll never get water through it. And we can't plant it like it is, in those clods," says Harold.

It's silent for a moment.

"Thirty-ten, or pickup?" I ask, wanting to know which to hook to the pipe trailer.

"Pickup," says Harold.

Bob and I look at each other. Raymond is out of it. We drive Harold's pickup down to the machinery dump and pull the irrigation trailer out of the weeds. The wind is blowing forty miles an hour out of the south now. We undo the wire on the posts that keep our miles of irrigation pipe from blowing away and in tandem we start loading.

We pause a moment, to commemorate the first load of irrigation pipe of the year.

"Which one first?"

Bob studies the pile, and points to one. The trick is to choose one that does not cause the pile to collapse. It's the same one I'm thinking of. And then we begin to stack the trailer in perfect unison. The right rhythm makes the work easier, and since the piles are built north and south, we miss the worst of the wind.

But we have to wire down the load so the wind won't take the pipe off the top, and then wire down what remains of the big pile again.

When we begin to lay it, the wind is blowing so hard in our faces it's a struggle to put a pipe down. The pipes are thirty feet long and eight inches in diameter, so they catch a lot of wind. Harold is driving. Which is why Bob and I looked at each other in the shop. We'd rather anyone else drive, even Raymond.

Harold never stops the truck in the right place, so we have to carry the pipe six feet backwards or forward. Harold can't drive the truck because he can't pay attention. He's thinking of his next move. Sometimes, he figures, it's just as quick to drive two or three pipe lengths ahead, and let us carry the pipe backwards. If we yell at him, he'll pay attention for a joint or two, and then go back to his old ways. We are resigned, and don't bother.

After we get a quarter-mile laid, the first three joints blow across the ditch. Bob tells Harold he thinks if he can get water in the pipe, and ridge up behind it with the blade, it won't blow away, but we already know what comes next.

"Get in," says Harold. He's through screwing around with this project. We're back in the machinery dump, loading steel posts.

Bob is a little angry now. He knows and I know that the wind is blowing so hard it'll blow spray over the back of the pipe and retard the water, washing out the rows. We have a bit of sense to us. We don't think it's a good day to lay pipe. I am the person designated to try and talk sense to Harold.

"I know it's dry, and the clods need melted, but don't you think we could wait a day or so until the wind dies?"

Harold is being diplomatic today. "You're probably right," he says, "but it's out there now. We better save it."

Bob calls steel posts "stobs." These are special ones Harold picked up at a farm sale somewhere, old oil well rods with a heavy knuckle at the top. We get out our drivers, two-foot lengths of four-inch pipe with a heavy plate welded at the end and rough rebar handles welded to both sides. Bob dons his gloves. I am always forgetting mine.

We've thrown the stobs out of the pickup at thirty-foot in-tervals and retrieved the pipe which has blown away, and begin laying it afresh, driving two stakes into the ground behind each thirty-foot section. Harold even drives a few. He still has that look of determination he had when he was younger and physically worked. Bob is angry now. He's pounding in posts with a single blow. It takes me three or four.

After we have the pipe stobbed down, Harold thinks we might as well try to water, so he drives over to start the irrigation well. Bob and I each have an armload of irrigation socks — plastic tubes with wire hangers which go over the pipe. The hollow sock acts as a tube, and directs the water into the ditches. We've got ten gates wide open at the end to prevent the pressure from blowing the pipe apart. When the water comes, we'll start opening gates and clapping the socks on. When we've got sufficient water running to relieve the pressure, I'll run to the end and start shutting off the wide-open gates. I'm better at running than Bob. I have to run because Harold is still fiddling around the irrigation well, and he has the pickup.

"Checking the oil," I grin.

And Bob grins back, though God will make him pay for it later.

Bob is only half right about not being able to run water. Only a portion of the water refuses to run down the rows. Where the tractor duals have passed and packed the ground, the water runs fine, but elsewhere it blows back and puddles behind the pipe, ruining the rows. With dutiful shoveling in the cold wind, which grows colder with the day, some progress is made.

It looks like in twenty-four hours the water will go about halfway down each half-mile row. Harold thinks we ought to lay pipe across the middle of the field, at the quarter-mile mark, shortening the water run, and Bob and I look at one another again.

In the morning the wind has picked up even more and the temperature has dropped to twenty-eight degrees and we're stumbling across the middle of the field with two joints of pipe, our boots sinking in mud where the water has reached.

We're in our shells. It's misery. When we stumble, the pipe jerks cruelly out of our cold hands. Harold gets out and carries a joint just to show it can be done and then gets back in the warm pickup. And we get it laid, and stobbed down, and the water turned on, as the spray comes over the back of the pipe and freezes to our clothes two inches thick.

When I ask to go home and change, Harold acts like it's a plot to get out of work. So we have an argument, and I leave anyway. I return an hour later, cold, but dry. Bob and I resume fighting the water. The cloddy soil is so dry that even if there were no wind, it would be difficult to run water. Ice has built up everywhere and it's hard to walk. Sometimes I break through into mud and sometimes the ice holds. But we get somewhere. Gradually, toward evening, the wind goes down a bit. Bob says it's just taking a breath till later. Harold's thinking there must be a way to get a man to shovel after dark, but he hasn't found it yet. He's looking at me. We have to let it go for the night, keeping the wells running and hoping for the best, and clean up in the morning.

I'm frozen, covered again with mud and ice, and can barely raise my boots. Harold follows me to my place.

"Do you want some coffee?" Kris asks.

Harold is always willing to sit a moment at a kitchen table and talk. That's one of the things I like about him.

"Yeah," he says. He's as fresh as a daisy, already plotting tomorrow's work.

"No one else was irrigating today," he says.

I call to Kris, "Hey, Harold says we were the only ones irrigating today."

She starts laughing. I start laughing. Harold doesn't know why. He's hurt to be left out of the joke, and he's leaving. I'm so tired, I go to bed without supper.

That night, the wind takes another breath and blows a quarter of the pipe away. A vast frozen lake is spilled over the flat field. We wade into it, and put more stobs behind the remaining pipe, and keep those from blowing away. Halfway into the morning it begins spitting rain, and five days later, when it quits raining, we have three inches. We drive all over picking up our pipe, shaking our heads when we find one wrapped ("wropped," as Bob says) around a telephone post.

Somehow, in the rain-refreshed morning, it's happy work, even though we have to walk a quarter mile through mud to get some of the joints. It's nice to be right. It was too windy to lay pipe, and no one else even attempted it. But Harold, in his own world, is happy, too. Staking it down saved most of it, he says. All in all he considers it a successful operation, never realizing for a moment that the project was stupid from the start. But by then, he has another problem. It is too wet.

Forty more such days will follow before we get the beets planted. We use implements to dry out the soil when it is too wet, and water when it is too dry. We drag big land planes behind our tractors to level the field so water will run down the shallow ditches the beets grow beside, and we apply chemical and stir it into the earth. We take up pipe, re-dig ditches, and plant atop the ridges with a twelve-row planter. We put the pipe back down, and "water up" the crop. When the seedlings emerge, they are tiny and fragile and are easily damaged by dust blowing down the rows. So we cultivate to stop the dust. And if they survive three or four weeks, they are almost as good as made, if winter doesn't come early and freeze them in the ground.

a wrestling match to the death

I was old enough at twenty nine to know that the biggest problem in my life was my father. During the summers of my youth I had been a virtual slave to him. And after graduating from college, despite my aimless drift through life, I relished my freedom. Why would anyone go back to the farm?

But I wanted to stop my drift. I had Kris and it was getting serious and we could no longer live in dumps with any pride. And Harold was ceaselessly giving me the hard sell. "If you came back to the farm, you could drive a car a city block long," was how he put it.

But there was also a new tone in his voice, one which indicated he really wanted me back. "Someone has to take over the place," he insisted. "You'd have to learn, but it isn't like it was twenty or even ten years ago. Not that you won't have to put out sometimes."

"Why not?" I was thinking. My father had gotten older, the family said he'd mellowed. And sneaking into that equation was my feeling for the land. I found that roads driven slowly amid fields of green wheat in the spring reached wherever I went.

And I knew by now that I had a sneaking half-love for farming itself. Plus the profession of farming has certain advantages.

"You can be your own boss," I told Kris.

"What about your father?" she asked.

"I don't know. We'll have to see."

"Hmmm, hmmm," she said.

Of course I fooled myself. That summer I had worked and lived in sin with Kris hadn't seemed so bad. Harold had been an indulgent father. We drove about the farm and gabbed sometimes, and raided the watermelon patch together. In one summer I had learned a whole cycle of farming and could competently run any machine on the place. True, the work on the beets never ended. Even Harold admitted we were too busy. He was still adjusting his management techniques to the crush of work that the conversion to a modern irrigated farm entailed.

"Do you want to run those sheep, Bruce?" he asked me a hundred times. At that time of the year our thousand head of ewes were in the pasture with the rams and through the summer would simply graze, and make lambs. Still, we constantly had to interrupt potentially more profitable labor on the beets to take care of one or another sheep crisis. They had to be drenched (treated for worms and other parasites), they had to be sheared, coyotes got into them, the windmill quit, or the fences needed repair.

And Harold had sugar beet fever. How could he not have? He was one of the first to see the big money coming, and now had allotments for three hundred acres. And his health was failing, though he was only sixty. He was "down in the back" that summer — which turned out be degenerative arthritis.

"I don't want to stumble around in those goddamned sheep pens all winter," he said. "How would you like to raise some sheep, Bruce?"

"I don't see how I can do it. What are we going to be? An irrigated farm or a sheep ranch? I don't see how we can be both. It's the beet harvest. It can run right through lambing."

Harold could see the problem. We were committed to the harvest and shared equipment with another farmer, which dragged out the harvest immensely. He turned the problem over in his mind again and again. How could we be in the beet fields and the lambing barn at the same time? There was no solution. So he went for the money and sold the sheep — a horrible, sad day for him. He had for so long called himself a sheepman that it was like tearing out a part of himself. It also marked the end of the old ways. He had pulled himself from his grandfather's farm into the future, and this at the age of sixty. He was no longer a husbandryman, he was now an agribusinessman.

We gathered up the herd, and Mennonites felt the bags and checked the teeth and selected the best six hundred ewes. The rest went to slaughter. Dust swirled in the corrals the day they were loaded — the kind of day that makes you spit black.

He asked me one more time.

"Shall we really get rid of them?"

I knew what he wanted me to say. He wanted a resounding "no."

"Ah, Harold. How can we do both?"

The sheep were gone and that great event so consumed my father's mind that he left me alone most of that first summer. I took my learning from Bob. We got through the entire season, including the sugar beet harvest, and made more money than ever before, sheep or no sheep. I earned my three thousand dollar bonus. I married Kris in November, and with that money, took her to Costa Rica.

Harold considered this plain foolishness, but was willing to allow it. My sister Julene had been married for years, and had produced no progeny. My brother had never married, and it was becoming obvious he wasn't going to marry. So my father, wanting grandchildren, tolerated nearly anything from me. With his husbandryman's instinct, he was sure of one thing. Kris was going to be a breeder. If he had thought otherwise, I think he would have driven her off. My plan was for us to go for three months and return in time for the new beet season. Harold lectured me on waste. If I saved that money, in not too many years I could buy a quarter of land.

"We'll all be here slaving our asses off for you and you'll be laying on a beach," he said.

"Harold, we sold the sheep," I replied. He had not yet figured out what to do during the winter, though I think if I had stayed he would at least have purchased some feeder lambs.

My money was well spent. Kris and I lived in a shack on the beach. We walked and swam. Roy Carter, the crippled numbers runner and dope dealer, would find us in the morning and sell us our joint. It seems we never got anything done before noon. Our beds were a big hammock and a four-inch-thick foam rubber pad. By ten a.m. each day it was already warm. Sometimes we lay together in the hammock and at other times on the pad, kissing, feeling, giggling. We had exotic friends and beautiful beaches and adventurous treks into the jungle and parrots and hibiscus and palms with coconuts free for the taking.

We went to San Jose and called home at Christmas. My parents were still so mad they barely spoke to us. They didn't want to hear about Costa Rica. What were we doing off there when our place was the farm?

"Such shenanigans," said my mother.

We got back as we had planned and moved into the only available rental, a mobile home, which Kris hated. I hadn't spent all the money yet, so I bought a stereo, the best equipment I could get. This extravagance further enraged my father, though mainly all he wanted to know was whether Kris was "flagrant" yet.

Kris had long black hair and with her blue eyes looked a lot like an Irish colleen, and at times still does. She handled Harold with a kind of bantering hostility. "When I am, you'll be the last to know," she would say.

The season progressed and we moved to a tiny house in the country, closer to the farm. Harold was dreaming of building a huge hog barn at this time, and letting us live next to it in a trailer. Kris told him there was no way she was going to do that and his estimation of her dropped. He confided to Jasmin that he didn't think Kris would ever make much of a farmer. And he told everyone else, too, and the word got back to me.

But the little house was peaceful, and Kris was knocked up by June. We had a rough summer then. At first she thought she had been infected by a parasite. And later, when she learned the truth, she puked and cried and indulged in hysteria, as most first-time mothers do. At the same time, Bob and Raymond and I were in a wrestling match to the death with our 320 acres of sugar beets. It rained, it poured, it blew, and things broke down. We wrestled tires and pipe and mud, and when I came home I often went to sleep without supper. But I was determined to make it work. I wanted that money.

Harold watched Kris's belly grow, and he figured he had me. How was I going to support a family unless I worked for him? He started talking about his grandson.

"Maybe he'll take over the farm some day," Mother said.

Before I fully realized we were at war, Harold had begun to consolidate his gains. The summer before we had talked about what we would do. I at least had the illusion that I had partici-pated in the decision-making. But during the second summer I learned I no longer had that option. Even the simplest of conversations ended in argument.

"How many socks do you think you can run, Bruce?"

"Probably forty."

"Why don't you make it sixty."

We were running water down hundreds of rows and Bob and I did it all. We had it calculated to the hour when each field would be finished, and how to most efficiently and at the best times of day transfer to the next field. Carrying pipe in the morning is just friendly labor, and in the heat of the day, drudgery.

"It's all planned out. This way we'll be done Friday morning, and Bob will be done in the north field, and we can transfer pipe in an hour or so to the corn."

Harold might scowl then. "Put sixty on."

What choice did I have? In a hundred ways Harold let us know that he did the planning and the rest of us did the work, though often his plans meant twice as much work for us. Harold and I had truces but they never lasted, and throughout the summer the arguments grew.

Finally he began treating me with open scorn. "The trouble with you," he said, "is that you just don't like drudgery."

In the shop, discussing the afternoon's work, he would ask me in front of Bob and Raymond, "Now, what does little Brucie figure we should do?"

"Blow it out your fucking ass," I'd reply. Such hostility seemed to make him happy. He would grin at me the way he must have done years ago when a hired hand had challenged him in the sheep barn and Harold had made the man eat sheep shit before letting him up. Someday, I thought, I'll have to eat the shit too.

I knew my work. It was my refuge. At least when I was hauling socks at the end of the day or in the morning, I could be alone and enjoy the weather. Sometimes, after making a set, I would sit in the pickup for ten minutes smoking a cigarette and listening to a song on the radio before plunging back into work. Harold always seemed to materialize at such moments.

"Why are you sitting here when everyone else is working?" he would want to know. There was no place to hide, even for a moment. Harold was always watching.

Beet harvest went on for weeks that year. The deal was, we'd help the Houses, and when we were done there, they would help us. We raced against an imagined early winter, which could freeze the beets in the earth and make them worthless. Altogether, there were a thousand acres. We ran our trucks and the Houses theirs, and as many more were provided by Tex–Mex custom haulers.

The Houses were Harlan and his son, Harlan Dale. Harlan stumped around his farm like Ahab on the back of the White Whale. His son, Harlan Dale, was a whirlwind of shop tools and welders and cutting torches. He worked until two a.m. to fix what had been broken in the fields during the day. Oh, why didn't Harold have a son like that?

Harlan ran the digger and I drove the topper, the field job requiring the least skill. I had been given ten minutes of training on the digger, but Harlan Dale quickly shook his head and gave up on me in disgust.

But I was a magnificent topper driver. My strategy for getting through it was to drive the topper as carefully as possible, hoping it would never break down so I would not have to suffer the humiliation of having Harlan Dale fix it for me. I carried a little brass pipe in one pocket and a film can of pot in the other, and usually by the end of the day the can was empty.

Our leaders do not know it, but if they would just furnish the world with marijuana, all the mindless, repetitive work would quickly be done, and with absolutely no rebellion. Little things ceased to bother me. I attuned myself to the sound of the flails and the engine and could tell by the slightest flutter or grunt when something was going wrong. Most things could be fixed by tightening a bolt if the problem was caught early enough. Even I could tighten a bolt.

Just looking at me could gall my father. I was bearded and cut my hair only once a year. What is the point of being a farmer and *still* having to cut your hair, I would ask. Harold would shake his head. My thinking was simply so wrong he couldn't believe it.

Earlier in the summer I had received a share of the wheat harvest. "Get a new pickup," Harold had generously advised me. He even gave me a day off to buy one.

I drove back from town in an old 1950 Dodge flathead. It was rusted orange in color, but stood straight up on its springs. In all of my life this was one of my most beloved possessions. It had a tiny turning radius and a hydraulic transmission, which allowed amazing control of the power. Harold hated the sight of it.

"Oh, my God," he said when he saw it. He may have been feeling sorry for me, for having been beaten out of the money.

When Bob saw the truck he grinned from ear to ear. "Why it's just like the one my dad had," he said.

But Harold was under the influence of the cult of the pickup. A man, by God, was what he drove. The antique Dodge was another affront to a way of life.

Though the pickup faithfully hauled me to work each morning by six a.m., the Houses didn't like it either. It was an impertinent little symbol of hippie freedom among the deluxe cab Chevy Silverados, and worse yet, I had plastered it with "Bill Roy" stickers. It was an election year, and Bob Dole was in the closest race of his life. Many Kansans couldn't forgive his support of the war, though he was busy weaseling out of it. The Houses were passionate Republicans. They couldn't stand it. They ripped my stickers off.

But we got the job done, at last. One thousand acres of sugar beets, 320 of them ours, the year the price went to fifty dollars a ton. I got another nice bonus. With that, and the money I hadn't spent on a new pickup, I had ten thousand dollars in the bank.

By now, it was early December. Kris had subsided from hysteria into a calm bliss. I lay in bed with her and felt the kicks, and sometimes I would blow on her belly and she would giggle. The work was easier now. I sanded down the old pickup and painted it yellow. We worked on machinery, and I began building a boat in my garage.

The baby was born in February. We named her Abigail Jane. Harold came to the hospital. The first time he held the baby he picked up her gown and checked the sex himself. He thought we might have been teasing him. His face registered a mean disappointment. I hadn't even done this right.

Then we were at the beets again. Harold was now sure he had won. He began striding into our house without knocking, wanting to know how the baby was doing. Kris was almost in tears.

"It's like he wants to catch me mistreating her or something."

I jumped him about it. "Do you really think you own that baby? That's our baby, Harold."

He acted as if I were insane.

"Do you own me, too?"

"Well, of course I do," he said, his effort to make this sound like a joke falling a little flat.

Our arguments early that season were unceasing and Bob, too, was caught in the fallout. Though we did the work, we could plan none of it. If we started farming, Harold would take us from the tractors to lay pipe. After we laid the pipe, Harold would find some excuse to take it up and move it. Getting rid of those sheep had been a blow to him. It hadn't been his fault. He had been talked into it. Now he was determined to take complete charge again.

All winter, during odd moments, I had worked on the boat. I had ordered it as a kit which came as little more than some ribs and plywood forms, some brass screws and a piece of canvas. It must have been May or June before I finished it — seventeen feet of double-walled canvas on spars and ribs of spruce, lovingly glued and fitted. Harold couldn't see why anyone would want a boat like that. "Where's the motor?" he wanted to know.

I had been working several weeks without a day off when it rained. It was too wet to farm. The day was a nice one. The boat was finished but untried. Harold came into the yard. I think our exchange that day went something like this:

"Hi, Dad. The boat's done."

He took one grumping look at my useless project.

"Since it rained, I'm going to take it to the lake and try it out."

"We need to dig a line."

"I'm not going to dig today. I'm going to try out this boat."

"You get your ass in the pickup. The rest of us have to work."

I knew that wasn't true. Nothing was so urgent it couldn't be put off.

"I've spent months on this and I want to try it."

"You ain't going to get any time off."

"Maybe that's the trouble," I said.

"What's the trouble?" he said.

"Maybe I need a day off. Maybe I need a whole week off. Maybe I'll just take the rest of the fucking year off."

I was probably screaming by now. He said something about how my pay was going to be docked. I knew how mad he was. He was thinking about teaching me a real lesson, of how he'd like to have me down in the barn eating sheep shit. But that might lead to a real break. Besides, he knew how strong I was now. It might not be so easy. He drove off.

I told Kris I wasn't going to work for the son-of-a-bitch anymore.

"Good," she said.

I went boating. It was a wonderful day, and a wonderful boat.

Harold came back on Monday, expecting me to go to work as usual.

"Harold," I said. "You don't understand. I'm not going to work for you. I'm not going to work for you ever."

"Ah, get off your high horse, and get in."

I almost did. But it was the look on his face that tipped the scales the other way. It was the sick look of a man losing something he thought he owned. It was greed I saw there, greed for my young body and my good eyes. "But I own you," his expression said. If I worked for him any longer it would become true.

"No way," I said. I shook my head. I could tell by his eyes he was starting to get worried. Maybe I did have some backbone, he was thinking.

He came back a few days later, wondering how I was going to support my family.

"I'll write," I said.

His face became a mask of sarcastic mirth. "You're nothing without me. You'll starve. You're nothing. I made you." He had said it out loud this time. He was raving.

I waved his words away and turned my back on him.

off the farm

I managed a credible escape from the farm, but this isn't a story about newspapers so I won't write about the twenty years I worked on them. I'll just say I learned geography.

Harold drifts in and out of these years like a wraith. At first, I kept my body lean despite the sedentary work. Instead of scooping, I rode bicycles and played tennis and, in the spring, not able to help myself, planted gardens.

On my few trips home, relations were strained although at times we could still laugh over the kitchen table. Harold was getting older, and the farm was getting better. The ditch irrigation was slowly abandoned and circular sprinklers were installed. The machines got bigger, and the fields were farmed cleaner. When I drove around, I realized how much the country had been tamed. Each year, more and more land was utilized. Whole roads disappeared to become trails among quarters.

The neighbors, when they saw and recognized me, shook their heads. It was obvious they thought me a fool, and suspected my father supported me. How could anyone walk away from a bowl so rich? My friends who had stayed on the farm pitied me, I think. I think they thought I was a half-wit.

I helped Jimmy Shaver's dad cut wheat several times. It felt good to feel the old heat and harvest, and I felt regrets about the slow life I had given up. Farming promotes a simple congress with nature you can't get in a newspaper office.

I knew from my sister, who was home for a time, that my parents were bitter. She told me that they talked at the dinner table about how Kris was to blame. She reported that Harold often spoke of "that damned woman who ran Bruce off." Just as often, he blamed me. I had no gumption. I had almost reached the status of a Benedict Arnold. I was a traitor. I picked this up myself on my rare trips from South Dakota. And I confess, I rubbed it in a little.

"Are you going to disinherit me this year or are you going to do it next year?" I would ask Harold, after hearing another tirade about coming home for good.

I had one glorious opportunity to rub it in when Harold called me to help at harvest. This must have been in about 1982. He planned an all-family reunion, as both Clark and Julene were also to be home for harvest. I took all of my vacation. Our relationship had mellowed a bit now, but he had not given up. He would call us, not often, and we called him and chatted a bit. He had no comprehension that we were comfortable. He visited us rarely, and judged us by what we lived in and our cars. His concept was that we eked out our lives in grinding poverty, so he always tried to lure me with tales of all the money he had made. Each call announced the acquiring of another hundred thousand dollars. OK. I was impressed. I did think at times of all that money, and how I had walked away from it. He told me if I helped him he'd probably give me that pickup he'd been promising me for years.

"Ha," my wife said.

"That's worth six thousand dollars," I told her. I am my father's son. It made me greedy. I'd sell it as soon as I got it and put the money in the bank.

"Ah, you work a couple of weeks and see. I can stand it that long. It'd be interesting just to see how it comes out. I wonder how he'll screw us?"

Kris laughed. I'd gotten her.

But when we got there with the kids, the Shavers wanted help. I counted the men and the jobs to be done and I could see through simple mathematics that my father had no real need of me. He only wanted someone to clean the bins and move the augers. More, he wanted the whole family together again, working together as we had in earlier days. But I wouldn't give it to him. I told him I was going to cut for the Shavers.

"The pay's too good. And they need me."

My father's jaws clenched and his eyes got big just before he got mad. It was like he couldn't believe it — treachery.

"But I need you here."

"Naw, ya don't. I counted it."

He would match anything the Shavers would pay. He'd pay more.

"They can't go without me. They got no driver. Besides, I don't know how much they will pay until it's over."

This is called negotiation. He named some niggardly sum, and then hinted if I would work for him, I might be getting a big bonus.

I told him no.

I chewed my cheeks in the enjoyment of it the two weeks I drove for the Shavers. I came home later than Harold and Clark, and happily pointed out that some people just did not work at harvest.

I'd gotten to Harold. He was reduced to threatening to charge me board.

"Are you going to charge me board? Are you going to charge the grandchildren?" Kris snorted. She was helping Jasmin in the kitchen.

Even Harold must have appreciated his position. A man with humor is able to step into his own shoes.

"I'll let Abby stay," he'd say, half-defeated. But he remained mad as hell at me.

When it was over, I was proud. I'd stood the heat and the dust again, over staggering hours. My machine had cut well, and I had not had a single breakdown. I'd cut steep gullies at sundown, when the light is at its worst, and had dipped the header into the honeybowls behind the terraces. I made a thousand bucks.

Harold asked at the table how much the Shavers had paid.

A lie slipped off my tongue like magic. "Twenty-five hundred," I said.

He gulped. I could see the quick calculation.

That evening, my brother told me what I had already guessed.

My father paid Clark double what I said I had made. We laughed about this for years.

we get mellow

Despite my treachery, I knew I had Harold by the short hairs. I had the grandchildren. During my early newspaper years, I had at last done something right — sired a son, Josh. Kris worked constantly to smooth things over, bringing me Father's Day and birthday cards to sign. She reminded me to call, and was always on the phone to Jasmin, bringing her up to date. But trips home were still an ordeal.

It was usually the same. The slightly strained dinners, the familiar lecture about the farm and how I should be taking an interest as it would someday be mine. The lecture never varied. What I should do was come home and go to work. Everyone in Goodland thought the same thing. How could anyone walk away from all of this?

But as I explained to Kris on the long drives back to Montana or South Dakota, if I played my cards right, I would get it anyway. By now, Harold's health had begun to fail. His heart skipped, and he was on pills. One day, he passed out, and after a checkup, found out his cholesterol level was over four hundred.

Mom set to work on that faster than she could skin a chicken. Meals at home were different, now. Harold looked at the green beans fried in canola oil, the bowl of broccoli, turnip slices and carrots, the fish and the baked potato and shook his head, though nothing disturbed his appetite.

"My God," he said, "I used to think the best thing there was was pork chops, with the grease dribbling down my chin."

Mom harrumphed.

Harold's big-bellied days were gone. He was down from over 200 to under 180. He had stopped wearing bib overalls in favor of gray work shirts and farmer's blue jeans, the loose kind with a hammer loop on the side. He had always preferred a hat to a baseball cap, and when he could get them wore a gray cloth fedora. He really looked quite dapper. And his cholesterol, thanks to Mom, was lower than a marathoner's.

And he visited us, too, usually at Christmas or Thanksgiving, but he made it to Montana once when the weather was warm. I insisted on taking him on a canoe ride down the Yellowstone. The water was warm and I had him in a life jacket, so a spill wouldn't have really mattered, but it was easy to see he didn't like the tippy canvas-covered boat, the one we had fought over so viciously years before. We went through a chute between rocks and dropped two feet, and he clung to the edge of the boat. He was a man who hadn't had many canoe rides, and he was a hopeless paddler.

I maneuvered us behind the ledge to where water drops in a pool and cast a spoon in. I knew there were always fish there. I nailed a golden eye on each of the first three casts while he was still fooling with his rod. But he flicked the red and white spoon I had given him expertly enough. It landed at the base of the ledge, and immediately he hooked something. Whatever it was, it was big. He tugged, it tugged back, hard, and the line whizzed out against the drag.

"Goddamn it. Don't horse it."

I got him calmed down enough to play the fish, but it was a standoff. The fish stayed where it wanted to. I told Harold to pump a little, and gradually, the fish was dragged toward the boat as the boat was dragged toward the fish. It was like playing a log. When we got close, we saw it — a ten-pound channel cat with a mouth big enough to swallow a softball.

"Oh God, don't lose it," he said.

I shook my head. He was about to fall out of the boat.

He wanted the net on the fish, now, but I knew the fish wasn't finished.

"Just keep the pressure on."

I was really an expert with that boat. I dipped the paddle in and swung it around despite his weight and the pressure on the fish. I could tell by the way the tail convulsed that the fish had about had it.

"Bring him up," I said.

He leaned against the rod.

"Careful."

I dipped the net low and worked it under the fish and, when everything was perfect, worked it up and over like putting on a sock. I had to reach down and support the hoop as the handle was made of weak aluminum. I flopped the fish into the boat. The red and white spoon was hooked in a tendril of flesh at the corner of the fish's mouth, but the flesh was so tough I had to cut the hook loose.

Harold looked at the fish. He couldn't believe he'd landed it.

"What is it?"

"A big catfish," I said.

We got on down the Yellowstone after that. He wanted to show Jasmin. When we got to the bridge, I loaded the boat myself. Harold carried his fish.

He couldn't wait to get out of the pickup. He dragged the fish inside dripping on the linoleum. "Jas-man. Jas-man." (The emphasis is on the first syllable. It means she's to come running. I hadn't heard this in years.)

Kris and Mother entered the kitchen together.

It was the grin that melted me. That was a part of him, too.

Maybe the best part. It was his brother Wilbur's grin. It was the family grin. It was the grin they probably grinned after painting Great-Grandfather's beard. Given half a chance, Harold can have fun.

Women have a certain instinct about how to act during such occasions. Mother and Kris said, "Oh, my God."

I was grinning too. There, for a second, I forgot all the old animosity. We were happy. We whooped and tried to put the fish in the sink. "It won't fit," said Kris. This made Harold even prouder. He couldn't remember ever catching a fish which wouldn't fit into the sink.

"You caught it, you clean it," I told him. This was no bull-head.

"Well, how do you do it?" Harold asked.

It was still sunny and warm and quiet. I went into the garage and got a three-foot length of two-by-six and searched around in the junk for the biggest nail I could find.

Harold watched with great interest as I nailed the head to the board and showed him how to slice the skin around it. I handed him some pliers. "Just pull the skin down and take the guts out. You can't fillet a fish this big. You just cut it into slabs."

By now we'd gotten the washtub and the water hose out. I got out the big butcher knife and took the hammer and pounded the knife through the back of the fish, whacking off two-inch slabs. We might as well have butchered a pig while we were at it.

In an hour, we sat down for supper. Kris had rolled the fish in cornmeal and fried it in a hot skillet in a half-inch of lard.

Mom shook her head. "All that cholesterol," she said.

I noticed that none of that stopped her. The two kids, Josh about five and Abby eight, were screeching that they wouldn't eat fish because it had bones in it, and Kris was telling them they were silly, this was a catfish and there weren't any bones, and milk was gurgling out of the jug so fast it ought to have been metered.

No lectures, no farm talk, a lot of laughing, and for a moment at least, Harold and I had what we both wanted — a family.

I had ample time to think of such things in Montana. I believe that is where I finally grew up. I picked agates on the river and walked a lot in the breaks around the town. It is dangerous to go alone. The breaks are steep, and covered with loose scree, but I couldn't help it. I got addicted somehow to the country, the beauty of it, the smell of the trees. The breaks were where I thought. I let Montana play in my mind simultaneously with thoughts of my youth and my family. It was my own family, Kris and the babies, that taught me what I needed to know. Kids are what love is about. And it was crazy. It was probably no different for Harold. The old bastard probably loved me. But I wasn't betting on it.

i'm fine. why shouldn't i be?

Five or six years later, I was in South Dakota, the editor of a tiny weekly lost on the shore of a large lake. I'd played out my skein there. That December, Harold and Jasmin had visited and he wasn't right. At the motel, he paused too long while studying his checkbook to pay the bill. He seemed lost, didn't talk much, and slept in the chair in front of the heater most of the time. It was not a good visit. He still wanted me on the farm and railed about it constantly. When they left, Kris and I and the whole family sighed in relief.

My job applications were floating everywhere. Both of us wanted to get out, despite the old house we'd bought and then moved onto a new foundation and all the work we'd done on it. Where we lived now was a village without the grace of cowboys. It was all Dutch farmers, the mean variety who belonged to "reformed" churches. Even the Presbyterians were "reformed." For the most part, the people were OK, but set in their ways. The village life went on, but Kris and I were not a part of it.

And half the people hated us for what I wrote in the paper, which was only the news. Circulation was up.

At last, someone called. *The Hays Daily News* in Kansas wanted to interview me and for the next two weeks I paced the floor wondering what I would do if I got the job. All the work on the house would go down the drain, but perhaps some hope still existed that I could have a career. The truth was I had always wanted to play with the big boys, just like I did in District No. 9.

I wanted to write for a metro daily. *The Hays Daily News* was far from a metro, but was a possible stepping stone. And, my God, anything would be better than covering another season of Herreid Yellowjackets and Pollock Bulldogs.

I combined the interview with a vacation. Every now and again, I have to wander. After the interview, I called *The Hays Daily News* from a Nogales, Arizona phone booth to find out if I'd gotten the job. I could see traffic crossing the Mexican border.

"You've got it," said the managing editor.

I told him I wanted to think about it for a day, but I already knew that I was going to take the job. Across the street from the phone booth was the paper I really wanted to work for. The press room was open to the street and flywheels as big as combine drive wheels were turning. A bank of bald men in green visor caps were pounding diligently on Linotypes. The paper was a throwback, maybe the only lead-type daily left in America. But I didn't go in.

The job offer ended my vacation. So much to do. I headed from Nogales toward South Dakota. I planned to travel up the spine of the mountains, but after a day of such driving I was sick of it. I plotted the fastest route to the Plains and found the straightest road to home. It was only an accident that the road passed through Goodland. It was almost dusk when I reached the town.

Mother came to the door. She was wringing her hands. "Something's wrong with your father," she said. "He's lost his mind."

I went inside. Dad was sitting in the easy chair as usual, happily reading the telephone book, but the book was upside down.

What followed was a nightmare. We took him to the doctor in Burlington, Colorado, who instructed us to see a neurologist in Denver. All of this took at least a day, and another night with Harold at home. He wouldn't eat. He came to the dinner table but only stirred his food. We didn't know what to do.

"What if he's like this forever?" my mother said.

I didn't know the answer.

The neurologist was a clock collector. I guess he kept them because he was impossibly rich from his trade, or maybe he just liked to remind people that time runs out. The clocks ticked for three hours while we waited. At last he saw us.

"What's two times two?" he asked Dad.

Dad concentrated.

"Why, five," he said.

Harold didn't know my name. He didn't know his own name.

"He's had a stroke," said the doctor, and turned to Mother. "You'll have to get power of attorney."

Harold was taken to the hospital for tests. We settled down in a motel to wait. My sister arrived from Arizona, and my brother from California.

Harold lay calmly in his bed, looking most of the time at the ceiling. He didn't seem distressed or even ill, but he couldn't talk. Once or twice he said something, but it made no sense. We'd all been given the pamphlet on aphasia. Clark drew a sheep on the blackboard, and a tractor.

"Do you know what those are?"

Harold didn't know.

Mother was drawn and white. Three or four days passed. At last, I could wait no longer. I headed back to South Dakota for my last month at the *Prairie Pioneer.* Since my car was still in Goodland, I had to take the bus from Denver and Clark took me to the bus station.

"I guess it's all over," I said. I shook my head.

"It sure looks like it."

"What are we going to do?"

"It's more what you're going to do. I'll go back to teaching. When I got the call, I considered not coming. Sometimes I'd like to just forget this whole fucking family."

"But you can't."

"Yeah, I know."

"Ah, Clark," I said. "It wasn't that bad."

"Yeah, I know."

I dropped my suitcase and opened my arms and before I knew it I was hugging my big brother and he was leaning against me.

I drove straight through from Goodland to South Dakota. When I got there, I called the hospital. A nurse answered. "How's my father?"

"Why don't you ask him yourself?"

I was surprised. The doctor had told us he'd be a vegetable for life.

"Dad?"

"Bruce?"

"Yeah, it's me. How the hell are you?"

"I'm fine. Why in the hell shouldn't I be?"

julene brought him out of it

But he wasn't all right. When he got home, he sat in his chair for days and sometimes got tears in his eyes. Mother whispered to me that his brains were scrambled. On one visit, he tore the house up looking for some old rifles he'd given me years before, which I had sold. The barrels were bent, and they had been worthless except as decorations.

I didn't think he'd last the summer, and I did something then. I took his old copy of *Sheep and Wool Science.* I didn't think he would be needing it anymore. I wanted that piece of him. I wanted to read the notes he had scrawled in the margins. I think in turn my sister stole it from me. It was a mistake to have done this. He went searching for the book one day and had a big fit when he couldn't find it.

The doctors used every kind of machine they had, trying to find the damage in his brain. They didn't find anything. His carotid arteries were clear. No pea-size spot glowed red in the CAT scan, showing where the tissue had died. Maybe he hadn't had a stroke at all. Mother might have been right. Maybe his brains were just scrambled. But we all knew something was terribly wrong because he had lost interest in the farm.

My mother says it was Julene who brought him out of it. She stayed with them through the crisis, with her new son Jake. Harold would sometimes just sit in the chair and cry, she said. We'd never seen him shed a tear.

"Julie got him out of his chair, and started taking him to the farm," my mother said. "He started coming out of it after that."

To tell the truth, I liked him better after the stroke. He seemed more human. He'd watch Jake playing on the rug and would grin as big as he had when he caught the catfish. He visited us, took a walk and got lost. We searched the whole town and found him unconcernedly sitting on a porch step, chatting happily with a five-year-old.

Music became important to him. When he was a boy, he had played a mean piano duet, "Under the Double Eagle," with his brother Wilbur. Perhaps it all came back to him.

My mother was half deaf by now, but he'd play the stereo so loud she claimed he was driving her crazy. Whole symphonies would play in his head, he said. He could hear every instrument.

And he traveled in the past with joy. He'd close his eyes and be thirteen again, playing with his brothers. The memories came back in great detail. "It's just like I'm there," he swore.

I don't think the doctors have a word for whatever happened to his mind. The medical profession has a whole vocabulary to describe the mind, but outside of a little anatomy I doubt they know any more than anyone who takes the time to think about it. Maybe the guy just needed a vacation.

Seeing that he still had something to work with, the doctors prescribed therapy, so my father sat with a calculator working problems in a third-grade primer, grinning when he got them right and frowning when he got them wrong. Later he said he decided he just wasn't going to be like that.

We had family conferences. My sister Julene put an ad in the *High Plains Journal* asking for resumes for a farm management position. No one had ever thought of doing that before. Of course, Dad still had a hand in the hiring and simply selected the first couple he liked.

He got stronger and smarter, but the new hired couple thought he was on the ropes and tried to parlay that into a raise. They had misjudged him. He fired them on the spot. I knew then that he was his old self again.

A year later he claimed another farm crisis and appropriated my vacation during harvest. It was hot work, and I had forgotten most of what I once knew, but I got through it.

"How much time you got?"

"Another week, but I hate to use it all. It's the only time I have off all year."

"You got weekends, don't you?"

Nothing ever changes. The farm was all important. I railed to my wife about his insensitivity, just like a whining teenager.

But when I thought about it, I was proud of him. The old bastard was back to normal.

clark

Harold called me in August of 1989.

"Clark was killed," he said. "You better come home."

"How?" I asked.

Harold said he'd been run over by a truck while bicycling on Highway One in California. There wasn't much more to the conversation. I slumped into a chair and stared ahead in shock.

"What happened?" my wife asked.

"Clark was killed. He was run over."

"I know, I know," she said. She was hugging me. "Yeah, I know."

I had heard my brother Clark say the same thing so many times. "Yeah, I know." It was his anthem of resignation. It was his dismissal of an inferior being — me — who couldn't possibly tell him anything new. It was his constant statement of his superiority, despite his enslaved condition on the farm.

We didn't make many pictures then, at least pictures you could see. But a few professionally made photos of Clark, our sister and myself hang faded on the basement wall in our family's now aging brick dream-home. In one of these Clark and I are together. He must be about ten. My feet dangle six inches off the floor. His hair is cut short, and he is staring ahead, serious and resolute, while I have an impish grin on my face.

I remember when these photographs were first made; I stared at them for hours. It was different from looking in a mirror. I couldn't find much to admire in my own image. I saw an impertinent little shrimp sitting in the chair with my brother. But he was big and strong and serious and handsome. He was going places. That was easy to see. The photo was proof.

Even my father saw it. "He's gonna work himself right off the farm," he worried, never guessing why.

Clark's second favorite phrase was, "I'm going to get out of here." And he did, as completely as any boy has ever left a farm.

If anything doomed Harold's desire that his sons take over the farm, it was education. Harold had gone to the university, and it was naturally assumed we would go to college, too. Here was the crack in Harold's will that my brother could exploit. From ten onward, day by day, Clark worked toward his escape. And just to make sure that no one would jerk it away from him just as it came within his grasp, he tucked away his 4-H money and studied as the others scoffed at him, and became valedictorian of Goodland High, and the scholarships rained down.

When he walked out the door to get in his proudly kept '53 Ford, he smirked at me. "You ain't ever gonna get out of here," he said.

"Yeah, I know."

I was now the one chosen by my father to be the farmer and the pressure was on. I don't know how many times I was told this, when dreaming out loud about becoming a doctor or a scientist or a philosopher — told I was nothing but a goddamned farmer and to forget about it. But I never learned. I could not repress myself.

My brother was all repression and squeezed himself to the point where he never came out of it. He marched as resolutely

through college as he had through a day's John Deere-driving
and through high school. He was teaching three months later
and didn't come home much anymore.

But when he did come home, it was easy to see that though
he had become slicker, he was still the same old Clark. Driving
oneself, working toward goals, can have its costs. On occasion
he'd break down into the damndest fits, and then pout for days.
It was over stupid things. Harold said something to him, or he
didn't get the piece of chicken he wanted. But he'd get over it
eventually.

What cheered him up was talking about college and returning in the fall. He talked at dinner about the beer parties and his
fraternity buddies and sang dirty frat songs ("Beta Sigma Psi, we
are pissing in your eye, because that is what a Beta Sigma Psi eye
is for"). Listening to him, my eyes got as big as the supper plates.

Years later, when he was in his forties, those same fits would
return. He'd go along fine, he'd be getting along with everyone,
and then someone would order the wrong flavor of pizza. He
wouldn't eat it. He said he'd just skip it. He wouldn't eat at all. By
now even he could see he was being ridiculous.

"Ah, Clark," I would say, and josh him out of it.

"OK."

It is a tragedy of life that a vulnerable person has to put up an
impenetrable field. For years he had been crushed at any slight.
He might stand quietly when lectured to about a bent oneway
hitch or a broken hydraulic hose, but at night he would squirm
with guilt over it. "If I just hadn't broken that damned hitch,"
he'd say. He too, wanted to live up to our father. I'm convinced
this is what turned him into an insomniac, and that years later he
was still tossing and turning, thinking of old bent hitches and all
the other imperfect things he'd done in his life.

He moved up the teaching ladder, though not so swiftly, and
struggled later, trying for a Ph.D., but something happened to his

sponsoring professor, and a year of study was wasted. Not getting the degree, he said later, was the biggest mistake in his life. He taught junior college in Benton Harbor, Michigan for a while, and then suddenly was in Germany for years. He took thousands of slides, which for the most part were utterly without composition, but always in focus. Many of them are of himself, standing in front of a big BMW motorcycle. My parents visited him there once, and came back with comments on how much my brother had grown. He showed them a wonderful time, all over Europe.

"He never even threw a fit," said Mom.

"He just about did," said Harold.

"What do you mean? He was nice the whole time."

"Don't you remember in the restaurant? He got on me about the way I was treating the waiter."

"Oh, that," said Jasmin, quickly dropping the matter.

Then he was home again. He sent out hundreds of resumes and finally landed a job at Colby Junior College. He talked for a while of being so near to home, but he hated it. He went to Denver, to another college, teaching chemistry, and bought a condominium. He had a heart attack there, which brought us all up soberly. It seemed minor at the time. We visited him, and the first thing he did was to order a martini at the Red Lobster. He drank three or four, but he had quit smoking.

Soon after, he had ditched the big motorcycle and had taken up biking and swimming and running in California, where he taught at Chico. He lost weight, said how he'd never been in shape before, and shed his guilt about being fat and sloppy. I'd teased him about this, and now he was teasing me. "How much you weighing, Bruce?" he'd ask. I'd ballooned up to 170.

A few years before he was killed, he'd had his first accident while cycling. He'd been hit by a truck, but that time he was merely thrown into a ditch. One of his arms never worked right after that. And then he was killed, bicycling on Highway One.

This time it was a logging truck, and he was out of luck. In his autopsy, the pathologist reported advanced heart disease. The diameter of the arteries had been reduced to the size of a pin.

I wouldn't look in the coffin. I wanted to remember him alive and not waxed down. For weeks, even years afterwards, I'd be all right for a while and then break down crying. My refusing to look at him was not a good idea. He marches bigger than ever now in my mind. Tromp, tromp, tromp. When we opened his apartment his socks lay stinking at the foot of the bed. Life just stops with unwashed socks.

julie

My sister Julene arrived home for Clark's funeral to find me outside smoking. She no longer calls herself Julene. She has a new California name, Julie, to go with her capped teeth. She always hated the name Mother gave her.

"How is it in there?" she asked.

"It's the shits," I said, "but we'll get through it."

Julie, in adulthood, carries herself with an air of superiority that is unpleasant to me. It is the same supercilious smirk of her youth clothed in sophistication. I've always thought that her life should have taught her a bit of humility, and that she should remember she grew up playing in the same pigpen I did.

She too had escaped Goodland. She went to college, to the University of Kansas, and met a man, another Bruce. Oh, what a wedding they had, with Harold railing and screaming in disapproval. And to a landsman, Bruce couldn't have seemed like much of a catch. He was short and dark and couldn't even keep up with the men on a pheasant hunt. But he was rich, which is just what Julie wanted.

Her marriage lasted perhaps a decade, but before their breakup Julie had persuaded Harold to make a down payment on a California mansion for the two of them. Near the end of her marriage she took off on a spree, traveling through South America, eating mushrooms and visiting Machu Picchu. When she got back, she divorced Bruce and became artistic. She decided she wanted to become a writer. She had the means. The value of their California home had skyrocketed and she had a healthy settlement and freedom.

Her new career took her to Nevada. The desert, she told me, was to her a spiritual place. But the spirits must have moved her in other ways. She met a cowboy. Anyone could see the cowboy was bad news by just looking at him. His handsome face had not a trace of character. He wasn't really a cowboy anyway, he was a California transplant living the cowboy life. But he was a good-looking bastard in his cowboy hat and pants.

This new marriage was brief. The cowboy brought Julie back to Goodland in the pickup on which she had spent the last of her divorce settlement money, and dropped her off in the driveway broke and pregnant, along with a trailer and a horse named Henry. He left her there like a dog and drove away in the pickup.

My parents were so happy at the prospect of a new grandchild, they merely said good riddance to the cowboy and welcomed Julie with open arms. It was not to be a routine pregnancy, and ended with a Life Watch flight to Denver. My mother was in the delivery room, and she talked about nothing else for weeks. It was as if Jesus had been reborn.

My sister does have a good stiff spine, and this rescued her from further humiliation. Much to my surprise, Julie became a good mother, and later would earn two master's degrees from the University of Iowa. She writes now, and teaches. She was in Iowa when Clark was killed.

I cannot clearly recall my brother's funeral. I was so grief-struck I was numb. I went to our old farm and wandered through the rooms of the home where we had grown up. It had been abandoned. I sat for an hour in his old room, looking out at the view he'd had. I walked along the borders of the fields we had tilled, and understood perhaps for the first time what had gone on in my father's mind after the stroke. It was like I was a boy again, the memories came back so strong.

Harold as usual did not bow his head during the prayers, but at least he did not stare around fiercely. It was impossible to tell if he was grieving or if he just accepted it as another thing that happens. "At least he didn't feel anything," was all he would say. I looked at my sister and suddenly saw that she was in utter misery. I put my arm around my father and touched her shoulder.

mother

A few weeks after the funeral, Mother and I flew to California to settle Clark's affairs. We had once been very close, but traveling with her made me realize how far we had drifted apart. During college, I wrote her long letters relating every detail of my life. This continued through the Peace Corps, but when I began writing for a living, I stopped for some reason. She typed her letters, which were as much fun to decipher as to read. The repeat keys tripped her up. "Harold says the wheeeeeeeeeeeeeeeeeeeeeeeat (Oh Shiiiiiiiiiiiiit) will make fifty bushels," is a typical sentence. Each of the repeated letters is struck over with a slash. "I'm not going to retyyyype the whole damned thing," she once explained.

We had to wait at the airport in Denver and I pulled a volume of Will Durant's *The Story of Civilization* from my bag. I had been plowing through it for months.

"What are you reading?" she asked.

"The history of the world," I said.

"That's nice," she said, looking at the fat red volume. "I'd like to read that sometime." Then she looked at the floor. "Oh, damn." She was crying again.

"Ah, Mom, we'll get through it."

"I know," she sighed. "It's just . . ." She trailed off.

"Just what?"

"It's just not supposed to be this way. Your children aren't supposed to die before you do, damn it."

"I know."

Then she was snorting with laughter. "Would you look at that?" Hare Krishnas were parading through the airport. "Men in dresses."

Her mood rocketed from grief to elation. I decided to be stoic.

I don't remember which city we landed in, but I do remember driving the eighty miles to Chico. I quickly realized that if I was going to survive, I was going to have to keep up with traffic. It was on the road that I briefly lost my temper. Mother fiddled with the radio knob. The car was too hot or too cold, and she fiddled with the air conditioner. She wanted me to look at this or look at that, but my hands were on the wheel, gripping it in white-knuckled concentration.

"Shut up, Mother!" I screamed.

It was like I had hit her with a two-by-four. One son dead, and now the other impertinent.

"Jesus H. Christ, Mom. Look at the way these people drive. I'm just trying to stay alive."

A few miles later, I gave in altogether.

"We've been living in the slow lane all of our lives, haven't we?" Three rigs thundered past.

"We sure have," she said. We were laughing together again in the same private manner she had reserved for me and me alone when I was growing up. It made me feel special.

But the stress was only beginning.

Clark's apartment was lonely. He had no decorations, except for some latchhook portraits Mother had done, and dozens of certificates on the wall of his office attesting that he had completed this ten kilometer run or another.

Mother said she couldn't stand it. Would I take her to the hotel? "You won't feel funny sleeping here alone, will you?" I said I wouldn't. "I just couldn't sleep here," she said.

I took her to a hotel and returned to the apartment and went to work. It was with great curiosity that I went through my brother's things. He'd kept the pants he'd worn in the seventh grade. Before I had been there two hours, three women had knocked. They had all been Clark's girlfriends, they said. One worked for the Goodwill, fortunately, and I got rid of most of the clothes. One said I looked just like my brother, and hugged me, but looked at me strangely afterwards. My attempt at a California air-kiss had mistakenly landed on her cheek.

I saw immediately what we would have to do — box up the good stuff and ship it out, throw away the junk. I worked far into the night at his desk, figuring out what he owed. I whistled when I saw his credit card bill and was astonished when I read his bank balance. He'd gotten a settlement from his earlier non-fatal accident and he'd kept every penny of it. I found his insurance policies and added them to the assets. Under the desk I found a last policy, one of those given away free to lure credit card customers. My daughter Abigail was the beneficiary.

In the morning, Mother was refreshed. I told her what I had found and what we had to do.

"But where will we get the boxes?"

I do have city survival skills. I went to the nearest grocery and got them from the dumpster.

"I would have never thought of that," said Mother. "What will we do with all this trash?"

"Put it in the dumpster," I said.

Mother went to work packing. "I know how to do this," she said.

Then I would find her on the couch, staring at the wall. She had found some memorabilia, or an old letter, which revealed something about her son she hadn't known, or which caused her to remember something about him.

"Oh, Clark," she said.

"Get to work, Mother." And she would.

The big problems turned out to be his car and the cats — Avogadro, a big black neuter tom, and Annabell, a calico female. The car was a problem because we had bought round-trip tickets, but now we found there was no way to sell it unless we did the California paperwork first. You had to make an appointment with the proper department, and the next slot was more than a week away. And what would we do with the cats?

"Mother, let's just steal the car."

"What do you mean?"

"Just drive it home. Take the cats." Cats, it turned out, required airline-approved kennels, which cost almost as much as a ticket.

It took a week. Lawyers had to be consulted, shipping arrangements made, a broker found to sell the condominium. At last we were out of there with the cats. Every time we saw a police car, Mother eyed it, and chuckled after it passed.

"You act like old John Dillinger," I told her. In Nevada, she began fiddling with the knobs.

"I can't get a dec-e-e-e-nt station," she drawled.

It was too hot or too cold. I have to have air when I travel but when I opened the window she said it blew her hair. And we couldn't get a decent meal, something I also complained about. "Rural America," I said. "All you can get is pig slop."

"It isn't even fit for a pig," she said.

Back on the road, I found a good clear classic rock station. Eric Clapton was singing "Layla."

"That old junk," she said.

"Maybe you can find something you like," I said.

Clark had liked classical music and there were some tapes in the car. Mother put *Water Music* in the player. It drove me batty. I opened the window. "It's blowing my hair," she said. I was stifling. I turned on the air conditioner, but she was too cold. I adjusted the vents to blow only on me. She said she wasn't getting any air. "All right," I said, never raising my voice.

We made it all the way to Ely, Nevada. I felt a severe need for six beers. At the motel, she said two rooms were too expensive. The innkeeper said she could let us have a suite.

"Would that be all right?" Mother asked solicitously.

"Sure," I said. The suite had two bedrooms, one with a television. Mom said she'd take that one.

All right, I said.

We went out for dinner, and it was awful.

I made an attempt, anyway. I went outside, intending to go to a bar and get quietly drunk.

"Where are you going?" she wanted to know.

"Nowhere," I said, giving up.

"Don't you feel sorry for the cats?" she asked.

"Don't let them out. I don't know if we can catch them."

"They can't stay in the cage all night, cooped up like that."

"Oh, let them go, then."

Mother watched television and fell asleep with it blaring. Her hearing was bad, even then. I may have slept an hour. In the morning, she wanted breakfast.

"Let's just get out of here, and try at the next decent town."

"All right," she said, but as I had predicted, we couldn't catch the cats. I tricked Annabell with cat food, but Avogadro bounced off the walls like a molecule of gas in a jar, and then took refuge under the beds. He streaked by, I took a dive, and missed. "Now we can't even get out of here," Mother griped.

I wanted out of there too, more than anything. Then I totally lost it. "All right, goddamn it," I yelled. "You wanted the fucking cats to have a good night, and now you've got it. Fiddle with the radio, fiddle with the heat, nothing's good enough for you to eat. Well, I've about had it. I'm sick of it. I'm sick of Clark, and I'm sick of this goddamned trip."

Mother was staring at me, her mouth open.

"Well," she said.

I began picking up the beds, leaning them against the wall.

"Bruce, what are you doing? You're going crazy."

"I'm going to make it so the goddamned cat doesn't have a place to hide."

The big black cat was streaking everywhere now but made a bad mistake. It ran into the bathroom.

"Block the goddamned door," I yelled. She did it. The cat came streaking out, a black blur, but Mother was quicker. She bent over and pinned the animal to the floor with her hands. In her youth, she had caught frying chickens no faster. Before the cat could even think scratch, she had pitched it in the cage.

"There," she said. But she was still mad. "I guess if any cat catching has to be done, I'll just have to do it."

I told her I was sorry. I don't think she heard me. She was out of breath, bent over with both hands on her knees, whooping with laughter. "Darn cat."

"Let's go," I said.

She left a note on motel stationary. "I am sorry about the beds," it read. "But we had trouble catching the cat."

Two miles out of town she began fiddling with the radio knob. We made it to Glenwood Springs the next evening and at last found a good meal. We had blackened fish and two carafes of wine, and Mother laughed and looked like a girl.

"What do you think Harold would think if he knew we spent a hundred dollars on a meal?"

"Don't tell him," I said. She laughed again. She had never lived so dangerously. We'd be home tomorrow, and she was relaxing a little.

"Th–a–a–a–t cat," she said.

I felt better, too. We talked another hour, over wine. On this night, she had no objection to separate rooms, and I guessed why.

"Do you want to go out?" she asked.

"Sure," I said, "a few beers will do me good."

I had more than a few and called Harold. He couldn't understand why it was taking us three whole days to drive back to Goodland from California when you could make the whole trip in one damned good day. But mostly he asked about Mother.

"How's Jasmin holding up?"

"Oh, pretty good, considering. We finally had a meal she liked. But you know how she is. It's too hot or too cold."

I could feel my father's loneliness for her. In their fifty years of marriage, this had been the longest separation.

"That damned woman," he said. "She's just never satisfied."

the big tractor

On one of Harold's visits he slumped in my easy chair, arched an eyebrow like a poker player with a full house sliding a single chip across the table to keep the suckers in the pot, and asked how many days I was working now. I'd put five years in at the *News* and had done twenty in journalism, and now I was trying to write novels. I was working midnights as a weather observer and writing by day. This was a quest my father did not entirely believe in. He is like most who live on the Plains, skeptical of men chasing dreams. "What you should do is get into cattle," he said.

I tried to explain. "How did all of those books get into libraries unless someone chased dreams?"

"You could chase your dreams at night and farm during the day."

I had just retrieved him from the magnetic resonance imaging unit at Hadley Medical Center in Hays. One of his arms was not functioning well. In fact, he could hardly move it. In a day or so, the magnetic resonance image would be reviewed by an expert, who was to relay his opinion to my father's doctor in

Goodland on whether an operation was needed. The tentative diagnosis was calcium spurs on the spine, digging into nerves.

"Just weekends," I said. "They cut me back."

The eyebrow arched. He made that facial expression I know too well, the one which means he is about to file something away.

"What days?" he wanted to know.

Too late, I got that sinking feeling.

"Friday, Saturday and Sunday," I sighed, trapped. I cannot lie to him. So for the next several days, after he had returned to Goodland, a slight cloud hung over my life as I waited for the inevitable call.

He called on a Sunday, about midway through the morning, because he knew I was always home then. Something else he has filed away. He wanted to know if he had gotten me out of bed.

"Bruce," he said. "If you could possibly get away, we could sure use your help down here."

The pinto beans needed to be knifed, the wheat needed to be planted, the volunteer wheat in the summer fallow had to be killed. Ron's boy Joe had gone back to school. Of course Nyla was a big help, but....

"I don't have much time," I said, trying to fend him off.

"I thought you said you only worked weekends."

I was deep in the tangle of the plot line of novel number three. I couldn't figure out whom to kill off and whom to leave alive, or whether the maintainer driver would make it through the blizzard in time to deliver the baby. Maybe a few days away from it would unravel the tangle.

"I can be there Tuesday," I said. How could I refuse?

I arrived home on Monday evening. Mother had baked a chicken in a new utensil. When the lid was pulled off, the cooked chicken was displayed perfectly browned, held on a spit upright. Mom got a big kick out of that. Nothing pleasures an old farm wife like the sight of a skinned chicken standing up for dinner. Harold was in his easy chair, reading a paper, examining me over his half-frame glasses for signs of alcoholism or any other recent deterioration.

"Getting quite a gut on you, aren't you?"

He always says that. It's the same gut I've had for twenty years. I have a theory that he remembers me best at twenty, and has forgotten the intervening years, the years I have toiled clam-backed at my sedentary occupation.

"You guys get what you want to drink and come to supper," my mother announced.

Dad got his skim milk out of the refrigerator. He calls it blue john. I've been on the blue john diet too, for nearly a decade, but he always forgets that, so he's surprised when I pour a glass.

The meal was excellent, of course. At the end, we're talking, and Father teased Mother about getting himself a younger woman.

"That would be good for me, too," I said.

Mother snorted.

"Don't get rid of Kris. She's the mother of your children."

Harold was grinning his mean grin and his fists were clenched in front of him in anticipation. "Maybe you can find one that has a better job than she does," he said, reminding me of my secondary status as family breadwinner.

I just waved him off, denying him the satisfaction of getting what he calls a raise out of me. He loves to get raises out of people.

In the morning we lurched in the pickup toward the farm. At that hour, everyone is buzzing around Goodland in pickups, making stops at implement dealers, bulk fuel outlets, and hardware stores before heading to the farm. Farm women meeting Dad on the road waved and grinned the Plains grin, a toothy confident and open smile, known only to places where the land is flat and the humidity is low. Mornings are crisp, even in summer. You can't help feeling good.

Into the co-op, out of the co-op, into Shores Brothers, out of Shores Brothers, into the Goodland Greenline, out of the Goodland Greenline. Everyone greets my father by name, hustles to serve him. They know he is an impatient man. It's not exactly fawning, but the closest thing to fawning allowed in Kansas.

I have a friend who explained why people act that way around old, rich farmers. "No one's told them no in thirty years," she said.

But out on the road, it's hard to tell he's in a hurry.

I put my seatbelt on. "Don't trust my driving, Bruce?"

"No, it's just that after writing the obituaries of a hundred and fifty dumb folks who'd be alive today if they'd had their seatbelts on, I've gotten into the habit of wearing mine."

We travel along for another two or three miles when suddenly Harold brings the pickup to a full stop in the middle of what passes for a major highway in Sherman County, although it is paved with gravel, and he puts his seatbelt on. Good sense always makes sense to him. Even if it means slamming to a stop in the middle of a gravel highway. (I tell him he ought to put a sign on the pickup, like one of those "wide load" signs, only it ought to have his name on it. He likes that joke. He even laughs.)

We arrive at the farm, a twenty-mile drive from Goodland, where Ron and his wife Nyla are already busy in the yard.

"Let's see what the boss wants," says my father. He and Ron confer while leaning on an International drill. First they are going to drill the northwest quarter, and then head up to No Man's Land. My job will be to drive the Big Tractor. I can't believe it. Usually, I end up manipulating scoop shovel handles. It surprises me to be so honored and I am a little thrilled. My task will be to kill the volunteer wheat growing in the stubble fields so that it will not infect the newly sewn wheat with wheat streak mosaic.

The big tractor is a John Deere 8960, a four-wheel-drive affair, floating on eight six-foot-tall Goodyear Dyna Torque tires. The tractor is huge, green, with bright yellow rims. Harold is engaged in pumping 140 gallons of diesel fuel into the saddle tanks, a job requiring him to climb a ladder with his bum arm, a feat he accomplishes by first lifting a hand to a rung with his good arm, then clambering up after it. His grip is fine. He checks the oil, frowns, checks it again, frowns, checks it again, and decides on two quarts.

He tells me the Big Tractor is the best thing that ever happened to the farm. But I can tell he feels a little guilty about it. The Big Tractor is something he has gradually worked up to. Years ago, the big tractor was the Oliver 900. Later, after I had left the farm, he moved up to a 6030, and then a Versatile four-wheel drive tractor with a Cummins diesel engine. But they were just big tractors. This is the Big Tractor, the Cadillac. A better one isn't made.

His justification for buying it was so unlike him — it cost him $108,000. The Versatile was perfectly adequate for the farm, he explained, but had a rough ride. "It beat me to death," he said. His arthritis. And then the ultimate admission. Whispered, almost like a confessed weakness. "Besides, I just wanted it."

"Quite an indulgence," I said.

He shoots me that look. He realizes I'm joking. But he is looking a little sour because, to him, extravagance is the ultimate sin.

I follow him to the field. He's forgotten the field cultivator we are going to use to kill the volunteer trails to the right, so the wheels of the machine are in the ditch, and the tons of metal, hydraulic cylinders and folding wings bounce roughly. But we get there, avoiding mailboxes and overhead powerlines, and I am relieved.

In the era of big machinery one of the most common farm accidents is the encounter between a big tractor trailing a folding machine and a high voltage overhead powerline. Generally, the rubber tires prevent grounding, but the first thing a farmer does when a machine gets tangled with a powerline is jump down from the tractor and lean against the rim.

Dad folds the big wings of the machine down into the stubble. Heavy rains accompanied by hail, which utterly destroyed his fall crops, filled the old buffalo wallows in the field, so instead of taking an angle across the field, we start an L-shaped strip along the north and west edges of the quarter section, a square of 160 acres with two shimmering temporary lakes inside it. I notice there are no ducks.

He explained he doesn't know which direction is best with the water in the way so he'll just do it, and shows me what the levers do. Some shift among the twenty-four gears. Others lift and lower the three-point hitch or operate any of the three hydraulic systems. It's quiet in the cab. Cold air pours out of the vents; stereo music comes from the speakers if I want it. After he lays out the strip, he turns the controls over to me.

The Big Tractor is articulated in the center, steered by huge hydraulic rams, which push or pull the articulation one way or another. The universal joint on the power shaft is the size of a five-gallon bucket. He laughs as I founder this way and that and tells me I'm lapping too much.

I squeal like a teenager. "I know that. I'm trying to fix it."

"Well fix it," he says. He's grinning. He has gotten a raise out of me.

But after traveling only one round he tells me to stop, climbs laboriously down the ladder, limps the ten paces past the edge of the cultivator, and motions me forward. I get off to a jerky start. He shuts his eyes, shakes his head, shrugs, and walks away.

I am a child again, under a vast sky, driving a John Deere R over a vast field. The hawks are wheeling above; one drops, and picks something out of the stubble I have just disturbed, lifts, drops it on the road, and picks it up.

The Big Tractor is a symphony of smoothly harnessed

power. It crushes washes in the field I would have never dared cross with the Rs. The field cultivator eats land in fifty-foot swaths. By noon, I have nearly finished a quarter. By the end of the day, the quarter is a memory, and I have cultivated the corners from two 133-acre irrigated circles.

The tractor is as easy to drive as a Cadillac. The only difficulty is in getting the radio microphone back in the holder after Dad has called me on the two-way radio, asking me how I am doing.

A day later I have worked over a half-section (320 acres), a job which would have taken nearly a week with the two Rs my brother and I spent endless summers on, fighting off flying red ants. No ants can get in the cab of the Big Tractor. It's sealed against dust.

I get the job done and Harold tells me I can go home. He wants to know what I think of the Big Tractor.

"After a while, it's just like any tractor."

He grimaces. "Oh, don't say that."

I am smiling. We are lurching toward town. Again, he begins to justify his purchase.

"It makes things so easy," he says. And then he begins calculating, just as he did after the stroke when he was trying to relearn math. "This way, we can knock out all the summer fallow in a week."

Now he is working on the arm. He is not going to be like that. He's not going to be a one-armed man, which is why we are lurching.

He hunches forward, using the momentum to throw his hand onto the dash, then he extends his bad arm by crawling his fingers along the padding, a process he repeats all the way home. Physical therapy, as my father conceives it.

We go through the seat belt conversation again. He slams to a stop in the middle of the road and puts his on. "It's the last tractor," he says wistfully.

"What do you mean?"

"Usually we put about six hundred hours on it a year. A good tractor will last six thousand hours before you have to touch the motor. That's ten years. I'll be lucky to last another five."

ron and nyla

Harold said that having a stroke, or whatever it was, gave him an advantage. Since he had to relearn everything, he got it right this time. Following the stroke, he stopped worrying about the advantages versus the disadvantages of a four-wheel-drive tractor. The answer was so obvious he bought one, first the Versatile and then the John Deere. Having one eliminated so many hours of tractor work that he could concentrate on other things. He began investing in circular sprinklers, abandoning the ditch irrigation. He pulled the last pipe four years ago.

A neighbor had told him two decades before, when he was investing in land-leveling so water would run in the ditches, that he was wasting his money. "You might as well invest that money in a sprinkler. You will anyway," the neighbor told him. Harold will now acknowledge that the neighbor was right, but he still keeps miles of pipe.

His failing body has been accompanied by a mental transformation. Now it is he who doesn't like drudgery and plots ways to avoid it. Still, some things never change. I'm sure he waters too much. To a Plains farmer, water on demand is nearly a miracle, and he's never really gotten over it. The cure for nearly every problem, as far as Harold is concerned, is water. And he seldom learns anything from the neighbors. In 1993 one of the neighbors didn't water his pinto beans at all while Harold sent the sprinklers around four times. If the crops had been in fields side by side, you couldn't have discerned a difference.

His attitude toward the aquifer is practical. To arguments toward conservation he replies it doesn't matter, because there will be enough for him. He smiles when he says this. It's the joke of a man who does not want to think any longer about what farming was like without water. He would have made it anyway, but water made it so much more profitable.

And he's always doing things — that is, requiring the men who work for him to do them — because something might happen. He sends the sprinklers around because it might not rain, and drags the shallow cultivator over the ground because it might rain and be too wet to plant. Due to the sheer randomness of weather these tasks are wasted at least half of the time. In that respect he hasn't changed, nor can he be argued with. The farm proves that most of the time he's right.

My friend was right about him. No one has told him "no" in fifty years.

By now I have mellowed to the point that to most of his demands I am amiable. When he asks me to come and help, I do if I can. In every human relationship, a sensible person eventually balances what has been done to him with what has been done for him. The scale weighs too heavily. I can never pay him back. And helping out may have even been necessary one August when his heart almost quit from congestion.

The wheat needed planting, and the pinto beans had to be harvested. It's getting so something like this happens every year. And of course, I'm no good at farming anymore, because I have forgotten almost everything or am out of practice. The principles linger, but the practical matters have eroded. Like how to hook up a drill.

Harold has a new hired hand, Ron Boese. Ron, he admits, is not a pleasant conversationalist, and his wife, Nyla, will never win a beauty contest. What the two have is an awesome capacity for work. As far as I can tell, Ron knows everything there is to know about farming. He's a driven man, though. When the pressure is on, his face twitches a bit, his voice rises in pitch, and he has high blood pressure. I think he'll probably have a blowout someday, and then what will we do?

Harold says he's just wired differently, and he'll hold up. Ron runs on 220 volts, like an arc welder, while the rest of us are lit inside on 110, like a light bulb. It's Ron I have to work for.

I'm actually good at driving the tractor, after Ron hooks it up for me. I could, after several years of retraining, and if my father lived long enough to pound all the hazards into me, fill the shoes of Uncle Raymond, Harold's tractor dog. I doubt if I could get much further. I can't weld.

Ron has me do the simple jobs. I'm sure that's what he thinks of me. A man who would walk away from a pot like this has to be a simpleton. What I do is drive the Big Tractor again, preparing the land for sowing. I work in the pinto bean fields, too, pushing front-mounted implements which prepare the crop for the combine. (I won't explain these jobs. It's hard to put mindless repetition into words.)

Nyla sows our wheat. She works day after day, pulling an International drill behind our oldest and noisiest tractor. She's a short, wide woman with a weathered face. She shows me how to fold the wings of the cultivator, at one point straddling steel and reaching down to lift the hitch. I have trouble picking it up. I have to laugh. I secretly start thinking of her as Wonder Woman.

Ron is steamed all through the planting and the harvest. Harold, back from the hospital but confined to the house, is constantly calling him on the radio, telling him to watch out for this and watch out for that. We have a huge, new drill, a testament to what can be built with a welder and stock steel, but it is so heavy, and the conditions so moist, that Harold is afraid the press wheels are compacting the earth over the seeds and the sprouts can't come through the crust. Ron keeps trying the drill, finds that the press wheels leave behind a compacted crust, and tries somewhere else. About all he gets done is to fill Nyla's seed box.

When the job is done, Mother congratulates me.

"Well, Bruce," she says. "You've done it again."

"Done what?"

"Saved the farm."

I'm not going to feel guilty about puncturing my parents' pleasant dreams about that. I'll tell them who saved the farm. Nyla did.

my pickup

Two winters ago, when I started my pickup and learned I had not put in enough antifreeze and the block was cracked, I was crushed. Thirty-five years of vehicles, and I had never done anything so stupid.

Most good farmers, my father excepted, claim to be Christians. Few but the truly God-struck, though, pay more than lip service to it. Harold is just more honest than the rest. As my father says, they all believe as he does or they wouldn't be here. They believe in checking the oil and antifreeze.

This pickup, a piece of shit when I bought it, was no great loss, but now I didn't have one. I still live among farmers, in a tiny village called Schoenchen. Every man drives a pickup. Not having a pickup is like being a Hells Angel without a Harley. The reason I lost mine is because I violated the true religion of the farmer. I didn't check the antifreeze, and of course, I paid. What could be more instructive? What religion could be more fair?

Not only that, I paid and paid. My neighbors, who often wandered over to drink beer in my driveway, noticed the pickup had quite a puddle under it. Jimmy Shaver was the first to see. He always seems to be around when a twelve-pack is cracked in the garage. Other assorted reprobates, attracted by the aroma of beer, were hanging around with greasy hands from some just inter-rupted mechanical job.

"Your truck hasn't moved for a while," Jimmy said casually. It wasn't a question, just a flat accusation that hung in the air dis-guised as curiosity.

I flicked my eyes about, from one face to another. Justice was bland and waiting.

I could have said, "I dunno. Just quit running. I'll get around to it someday. Acted like the distributor cracked."

But Shaver would have said, with an air of mechanical supe-riority, "Let me take a look," and I would have heard from him how the block was cracked.

"Didn't you check the antifreeze?" he'd say, while behind him the grease-stained jury solemnly nodded.

Oh, it's just too droll. "I let the son-of-a-bitch freeze up," I said.

I saved Plains face. I had put some old antifreeze in, saved from the motorectomy of a Pontiac. "Must of been watered down."

I waited for it and got it. Shaver laughed his low "heh-heh."

I'd broken the faith. I'd mistreated my pickup. I would feel the weight of it on my shoulders through my entire life. In the fall, ten years from now, the memory of the Great White Pickup will surface. I'll shut my eyes and shake my head, wondering how I could have been so stupid. But I won't forget to put in the an-tifreeze again.

harold's pickup

I've struggled for years with a theory that most of us are encased in bubbles of time. We all listen over and over to those same old rock records. Somewhere back there we formed.

Take a hawk's view. Look down on the green squares of crops and the brown squares of fallow. Somewhere out there is a song I can't quite hear, or maybe it's just the wind humming through the power lines. On a dirt road a pickup travels trailing dust. The driver is my father. I'm along for the ride.

I don't know what he's thinking. He's got the window down and the air conditioner going full blast and his hand out the window planing the air. He's eighty years old. Hard to tell what's going on inside that head.

I know that from time to time he must pull himself from memories back into the present. For the most part, though, he talks about what he'll do next year. He's thinking about buying two more quarters, calculating the income from them against bank interest. Cattle worry him. He's worked over the corrals and set up for two hundred, but the price is too high. He's holding the beans. The price is high, thirty-two dollars a hundred, but he can't sell until after the first of the year because of income taxes.

From the congestive mishap in August he says he's been resurrected. Sometimes, however briefly, he'll stop talking about the farm and smile as he remembers something about Clark.

"Clark was so damned smart. When he was just a little thing, he could spell 'International.'"

I'm not so stupid. I grew up listening to Clark spell that word.

When neighbors came over Harold had him spell it. He'd spell I-N-T-E-R-N-A-T-I-O-N-A-L at dinner. Probably it was this ability which convinced Clark's early teachers they had something to work with.

It's funny how things work out. I couldn't be taught to spell anything, or failed to see the value of it. So forever, Clark was the intellectual, the smart one, and I was the jester. He was the firstborn and I was the fool who came along before Julie. Julie is what Mother said she always wanted — a girl. After Julie was born, Mother told everyone she had what she wanted, and wasn't going through that again. The children stopped. The Bairs were a balanced, sensible family. It was very Lutheran.

I have to pull myself back from my memories, too.

The pickup is brand new. It's a red Ford with velour seats and push button windows, an AM-FM radio with a cassette player, automatic and air and cruise control. I tease Harold about that sometimes. "A man could make a down payment on a quarter of land with what this truck cost."

I know he's thought the same thing more than once and probably said it about someone else's truck. He knows all about the Depression. He grew up in it. The farmers like him who survived and didn't forget are still around and have done everything possible to pound a single lesson into their sons. "Times can get hard."

But Harold has also started thinking he's got it made. He's figured it over and over and can't see any way he can go broke. After a twenty-year hiatus, he has again cautiously begun investing in land. He knows a good deal when he sees one.

But the pickup is different. "I can afford it."

He goes into his spiel about how he has to go to the farm every day, and he might as well have one little thing.

"Like a $23,000 pickup with red plush velour seats?"

I'm grinning when I say it. I'm glad he has it. Who's worked harder to get one? "Hey, Dad. Do you know what an extravagance is?"

He shows a little interest.

"What?"

"Something you do without until you find out how nice it is."

He smiles. He once thought air-conditioning was a useless frill designed to give only trouble. He and I both know now that such ideas last only through youth, when the heat is your friend, and end at about the same time it starts to sap your strength. In the winter, Dad wants the window up all the time now. He gets cold. The XLT has a good heater.

another funeral

As so often happens now, we get together at funerals. This one was my Aunt Irene's. Mother called and told me she had died.

"I guess I better come down, then."

"Yes. You should. But Kris and the kids don't need to come."

The family would be pleased if my small branch of the family metered out some sympathy, but no use gushing. It was that kind of funeral.

Irene's farm bordered ours on the north. I often walked across the pastures to her place where I would play with Darrel Pettijohn. Irene's daughter, Ruby Pettijohn, lived with her then, with her children Darrel, Mark and Susan.

I didn't think much about old times on the way to Goodland. I was only fulfilling a family duty, though I was mildly interested in who might show up and whether I would recognize them. I hadn't seen some of these people for decades.

"Here's Bruce," I heard my mother say through the window as I walked across the driveway. I figured I didn't have to knock.

It was absolutely no shock to me that a bunch of strange people was gathered in the living room. I was prepared for that. Bob Cook, my cousin, Irene's son, said "Hi," and offered to buy me a razor.

"Ah, you guys worry too much about hair. I've had this since 1962." I'm bearded and always have been.

What I was actually thinking was, "Fuck you." But how can you say that to a man whose mother has just died? So I was affable. And he was probably only joshing me. I sat and started talking to Harold, pumping the latest health information out of him.

"So you've been resurrected?"

"Pretty much."

"Hmmm," I said. "All the way?"

"Well. Yes. Better than before the fracas."

And Bob Cook butted in, talking construction. I believe he builds houses in Salina.

No one did too well at introducing all of us. What we needed to do was stand in a line and tell people who we were and how we were related. It would have silenced the whispers. But instead, introductions occurred in corners and didn't spread through the room.

"Have you met Steve?" A big hand folded over mine. I'd wondered who Steve was. He stuck out among the rest of us. He wore blue jeans, a work shirt, and tennis shoes. Most of us wore suits, or at least polyester.

"I'm Steve, Ruby's son."

"I didn't even know Ruby had a son named Steve."

He grinned, but ruefully.

"About how old are you now, Steve?" Harold asked.

"Thirty-seven," he said.

They had been hard years. He wore his blond hair long, but

he was balding. His face looked like a boot track in the mud, it was so plain.

"What are you doing, now?" asked Harold.

"I build fence," he said.

His face was tragic, but he was slim in his jeans. His belly was flat and his shoulders swung easily in his work shirt. And somehow, I didn't think this man was stupid.

He seemed most comfortable with Mark, Ruby's second son. Mark's face was all squashed behind a halo of graying wild hair. He must have been about forty-three, but he looked sixty. Three yellow teeth jutted up from his lower gum in an otherwise empty mouth. Most of the time he was outside chainsmoking.

Mark, they told me, had become schizophrenic. He lived in Denver with Ruby, and wouldn't take his medicine. Out for a smoke myself, Mark said he was moving. He and Ruby fought all of the time, he told me. He was going to Kansas City.

Inside I met a daughter I forgot Irene had. Harold introduced her as the Georgia Peach. Her name is Jeannette Baxley. Jeannette said she ended up in Georgia because Irene made her go to school. It was a business college in Denver, where she a met a man, and he was stationed down South.

"It really isn't the kind of country I'd choose to settle in. It's so hot. Last summer the humidity nearly killed me." She fanned her face a little with her fingertips, like a southern belle. I thought she looked like Grandma Carlson, but Mother said she was the spitting image of Irene. If so, Irene was once beautiful.

The resemblances ripped me out of the living room and back to my childhood. Aunt Irene lived in a house with her second husband, Fred Weise, a dour and dark-skinned man who somehow always reminded me of my Grandfather Ferd. My father always classified him as "quite a doer." The living room was sunken, which meant that whenever you entered it someone had to yell "Watch out!" Otherwise you'd pitch down the stairs.

Aunt Irene was heavy, her face severe, and she always seemed a little angry. She was a lot like Grandma Carlson in that respect. And the dresses she wore. One I remember particularly was shapeless and brown, with a big rip over one huge tit, through which a slip showed.

Mother would gripe at home, wondering why Irene didn't change that dress. The theory was that it was in sacrifice. Everyone always said she never did anything for herself. But it was also implied that she enjoyed playing the martyr. Irene usually wore flat black shoes and white rolled-down socks, which completes the picture. She was not a person a little boy could love easily. But it was she who took care of us whenever we had a crisis.

I was most curious about Darrel because he had been my friend, or enemy, depending on how you looked at it. He also wore blue jeans, but with a sports coat. I was surprised to see the tiniest paunch on him, he'd always been so hard-wired. He sported thin muttonchops, and something was wrong with his eyes. They didn't look like they were floating on much.

Outside, we compared snooses. His was Skoal classic, and mine wintergreen. He had the real man's stuff, he let me know. Then it was time for the traditional lying. He handed me a business card, almost with a conspiratorial air. According to the card, he was the proprietor of a "common law, private enter-prise, of the American Republic." The company was called Environmental Monitoring Services, and provided "Biological, Chemical, Sampling Analysis, Retrival, Desimenation Documented Destruction, Investigations, Couriors, Special Operations." I refrained from pointing out that some of the words were misspelled. I didn't know quite what to think of it. "Wow," I said, carefully.

Darrel was telling me how he was going to build a geodesic dome outside of Denver because where he was living was becoming too crowded. He had $100,000 equity in his house, he claimed. I was plotting how to gracefully escape this conversation. The call to lunch saved me.

By now, the house was filled and I studied the people. My second cousin Bob Cook was a wide-shouldered man in his thirties with a drooping handlebar moustache. His fiancée was a tall pretty woman, and when she stood a moment in the doorway, the light shined through the fabric of her blue dress and revealed a magnificent pair of legs. Aunt Ruby was as thin as ever, and missing a few teeth, and talked in a tiny, squeaky voice.

My cousin Alvin Rust, quite a bit older than I, and his wife, Betty, were taking care of their daughter Cheryl's identical twins. Alvin's big hands were very patient with them.

A young, pretty professional woman talked to me. She had nice legs too. She'd heard I was a writer.

"No, I'm sort of a bum right now," I told her.

I was never introduced to the two young people, one a girl with straight blond hair and the other a chunky young man with black curls. I assumed they were grandchildren.

Everyone discussed how Grandma looked. It was generally agreed by Irene's family that the undertakers had done a good job, but it didn't really look like her. "She changed her hair in the nursing home," said Mother.

Bob Cook said that the mortician had done a good job covering up the cancer that had eaten through her cheek. "It's a good thing it wasn't on the other side," he said. "You can only see a little white mark where it ate through."

"They can never get it right," said Jeannette. "They can't get the expression."

After we ate, I drove Mom and Dad to the funeral home. On the way Harold told me that Steve was a "catchcolt." I calculated the years. If he was thirty-seven, I must have been twelve when he was born. How could I have not known about him?

But then I remembered it was about that time that Ruby had moved to Denver. "They kept it pretty quiet," said Mom. "Then Susan did the genealogy, so they brought him out of the closet."

I winced over what I had said to him when I first shook his hand.

The funeral was sparsely attended, but outside, I saw Opal Seaman from the old neighborhood. Bill, her husband, had died years ago of a heart attack. Everyone was surprised. He'd always been so thin. Except for being almost bald, she looked the same.

"You still living on the same old place?"

Of course she was, she said. "No use letting a perfectly good house set empty." It was a little dig at us for abandoning our old house. Soon after Clark's funeral, a new owner had it burned down to save on taxes.

I inquired about her children. "It's Marvin, Brian, Matthew, and Dawn, isn't it?"

She was pleased I remembered all of the names. She told me where they were. Marvin, my old friend, was in Seattle teaching at a junior college. The rest were scattered all over the country, on the coasts. The whole family had joined the Navy after high school, following in Bill's footsteps. I had once written a story about them called "The Seamen of the Plains." Opal said she'd been so busy going to funerals lately, she hardly had time to do her grocery shopping. "When I'm gone, you'll be at the top of the heap, won't you?" she asked.

I grinned.

"Maybe I can surprise you and die first."

She whooped. I found that I now liked Opal better than I ever had.

In the waiting room, Steve leaned back in his chair and closed his eyes. I wondered if he was thinking of the family he had never really belonged to. Or maybe he was just hung over.

He looked like a hard liver. The phone behind his head rang constantly with mortuary business and he was annoyed when he had to answer it and then go look for one of the morticians.

The Rev. Dr. Tom Schneider did a good job, much better, I thought, than he did at my Uncle Johnny's funeral. He had taken the trouble to ask the family about Irene and wove her stories into his sermon about the father's house having many rooms. No one cried that much. Bob and Ruby seemed the most grief-stricken.

Irene, the Rev. Tom said, cradled her brother John for a year because when he was born his skull had not completely formed. She protected him until it did. My family still says that John was the most dynamic of the Carlsons, but years ago he was killed by lightning while driving a tractor.

After my Grandmother Carlson died, Mother and Irene didn't talk for decades. It was over land. The Rev. Tom told how Irene was such a good business woman, she balanced the books daily to see that no money got away.

"She met her match in my father," I thought. I smiled, thinking of that war, but quickly wiped the grin from my face in deference to the solemnity.

A few years ago, Irene called from the rest home and wanted to see Mother. She was half crazy by then, everyone said. The Rev. Tom called it "walking in dark clouds." When Irene asked to see Mother, Harold told her to take someone along. He was afraid Irene might hurt her, she was so crazy. Mom went alone anyway and they talked, and all the old animosity was swept away.

"It's like it never happened," said Mom. "All I need to know is that she's my sister and she loves me."

Before the land fracas, Irene had been like a second mother to her.

I didn't know until I read the announcement that Irene's

first name was Julia. Perhaps Mother combined the two in nam-
ing Julene. But there's a complication. Grandma Carlson's middle
name was also Julene, though according to mother, she kept that
a secret.

Maybe the big drought won't sweep us out of this country if
we continue to weave connections like that. Eventually, so much
history will have penetrated the earth the families will be as established as buffalo grass sod.

a song scattered in the wind

A tractor is conducive to thinking, unless one wears the wrong jeans. It's best to avoid tight pants. I've gone home to Goodland now so many times to drive the tractor it's changed my dress. I've discarded the tight Levis of my youth in favor of loose-fitting denims, an inch too big in the waist.

Last summer, I was home for thirty days or so, working through the crunch times. I can't say no. I don't even think of it. Harold is fading fast. He barely has the energy to drive to the farm and back. When he gets home, he sleeps most of the afternoon in his chair. The doctor says there's not much left of his old heart.

"He's easy to take care of," says Mother. "He never complains."

And he doesn't. "I don't hurt," he says, "that's the big thing." I asked him recently at supper what his plans were. "Why, to live as long as I can," he said.

The 1995 crop was one of our biggest ever, averaging almost sixty bushels to the acre. I planted half of it, and I'm proud of the job I did. We'll have to wait and see this year. I fertilized half our land, and planted it. Harold called me on the radio a dozen times a day during sowing. "Bruce, it doesn't hurt to get off the tractor and check the drill every now and then."

"Sure thing," I'd say.

I couldn't get anything done without Ron. I'm still incompetent. He helps me hook up and so on, but a lot is coming back to me.

Ron's not much of a laugher. If I worked with him long enough I'm sure I'd find his funny bone and begin working at it. But mostly, he's so hyper, I just want to work and pray nothing goes wrong so I won't have to ask him to fix it.

I got over a lot of land last year, daydreaming the days away. My father's life is mostly memories now, and more than half of mine is. It reminds me of what the mother of one of my old Sunday schoolmates said to me at a funeral. I was walking out, but she called to me.

"Bruce?" she asked, to make sure it was me.

"Yes," I said.

"Come closer," she said. She was sitting, and I bent to look at her face. She studied mine, and smiled almost as if assured she'd found something good there. It made me feel proud. She had the most beautiful blue eyes. They twinkled.

"You guys aren't spring chickens anymore," she said.

A farmer has to be the most constant thinker on earth. So much of the work is done alone. I know what Ron is thinking about because he calls me on the radio. He's thinking about farming. "When you come to the end, go down the corners first, that way you can come out on the road."

"O.K." I do anything he tells me to because he's almost always right. His suggestion will save fifteen minutes.

Still, I'm not much of a farmer. It's the loneliness that gets to me. Years ago I took a canoe trip down an Alaskan river. At the

end of two days I was beating rocks together just to hear something. Poor old Raymond, our tractor dog. I wonder what he
thought at the end of months in the seat of a machine.

But on the tractor, it all comes back to me — my brother, my
sister, Our Place, The Other Place. I admire what my father has
done.

Near our one rental quarter is The Place Where Uncle
Kenny was Killed, on the way to St. Francis is The Hill Where
Uncle John was Killed by Lighting, that low corner is The Spot
Where the Log Chain Broke and Took Off the Head of the
Hired Hand, the quarter I'm farming is where The Power Shaft
Caught Harold's Leg.

I respect the memories of the place. When I farm, I do it
carefully.

The fields are smoother now. The big machinery reduces
and smooths the knobs and fills the gullies. It's still good topsoil,
except perhaps on the hillsides, where the white gumbo shows
through like bones. Far off, perhaps a mile or two away, when I
reach a hilltop, I can see other farmers driving tractors, the dust
and the smoke slowly drifting with the wind. The one grace
Goodland has over the rest of Kansas is the air. You can see for
miles. It all looks in slow motion. Every now and then I break the
rules, stop the tractor, and turn it off. And far off, on that hillside
two miles away, I can hear the squeaking of an old drill, like a
meadowlark's song scattered in the wind.

A NOTE ON THE AUTHOR

BRUCE BAIR has worked for newspapers in
Kansas, Montana, and South Dakota. He lives in
Schoenchen, Kansas with his wife, Kris, and is
working on a novel based on his experiences as
a journalist.

A NOTE ON THE BOOK

This book was composed by Steerforth Press
using a digital version of Bembo, a typeface produced by Monotype in 1929 and based on the
designs of Francesco Griffo, Venice, 1499. The
book was printed on acid-free papers and bound
by Quebecor Printing ~ Book Press, Inc. of North
Brattleboro, Vermont.